SMALL SCALE INDUSTRIES

VOLUME ONE

Books in Series

Vol. I Problems of Small Scale Industries

Vol. II Management of Small Scale Industries

About the Editor

Mookkiah Soundarapandian is Reader in Rural Industries and Management, Gandhigram Rural Institute (Deemed University), Gandhigram. Apart from teaching and extension responsibilities at Gandhigram Rural Institute, he has been engaged in research activities. He has published many research articles in various reputed journals at national and international level and six books, namely, (i) Rural Industries in India, (ii) Women Entrepreneurship, (iii) Tribal Development in India, (iv) Industrial Resurgence in Rural India, (v) Literacy Campaign in India, and (vi) Rural Entrepreneurship. Apart from providing research guidance to a number of Ph.D. and M.Phil. students, he has directed and completed Nine minor research projects and two major research projects that were sponsored by University Grants Commission, Indian Council of Social Science Research, Bharat Gyan Vigyan Samiti, Ministry of Rural Development, New Delhi and State Resource Centre for Non-formal Education, Chennai. One major research project that is at an advanced stage of completion, are financed by University Grants Commission, New Delhi.

SMALL SCALE INDUSTRIES

VOLUME - ONE
Problems of Small Scale Industries

Edited by
M. Soundarapandian
Reader in Rural Industries and Management,
Gandhigram Rural Institute (Deemed University)
Gandhigram

CONCEPT PUBLISHING COMPANY, NEW DELHI-110059

ISBN-81-7022-989-8 (Set)
ISBN-81-7022-990-1 (Vol. I)

First Published 2002

Published and Printed by
Ashok Kumar Mittal
Concept Publishing Company
A/15-16, Commercial Block, Mohan Garden
NEW DELHI-110059

Phone : 5351460, 5351794
Fax : 091-11-5357103
E-mail : publishing@conceptpub.com

PREFACE

Today, Small Scale Industries form the backbone of a developing country like India. They have become an effective weapon in bringing into existence a harmoniously balanced integrated socio-economic order in our economy. The role of small scale industries is most significant both in respect of employment and value added particularly in the developing economics. At present, the industries scene in the country is competitive by the liberalisation policy of the Government. The proper management and efficient utilisation of local resources for the development of industries provide the way for their expansion and strengthening. It is the right time to dicuss the problems and management of small scale industries in India and to find out the ways and means for the promotion of small scale industries in India. For this purpose, a seminar was conducted by the Department of Rural Industries and Management, Gandhigram Rural Institute, Gandhigram.

A few important topics are discussed in the seminar. The topics analysed in the seminar are categorized into two parts. They are :

Part - I

Problems of Small Scale Industries : Availability and Source of Raw Materials, Inventory, Production Process and Problems relating to Marketing, Advertisements, Sales Promotion, Technical Problems and New Economic Policy.

Part - II

Management of Small Scale Industries : Management of Agro based, Mineral based, Textile, Forest based, Polymer and Chemical based industries, Training for the executives in the small scale industries, Development of Managerial skills for the rural entrepreneurs and other managerial problems.

These two categories of papers are presented in two volumes as: Small Scale Industries, Vol. I and Vol. II.

I am grateful to Dr. G. Pankajam, Vice Chancellor of GRI, Gandhigram and to Dr. N. Thillainayagam, Professor and Head, Department of Rural Industries and Management, Gandhigram Rural Institute, for their encouragement and support for publishing the books. The untiring support exerted by my wife Mrs. S. Indumathy and my children Diwakaran and Vidya, helped me to enjoy the completion of this work. Finally, my sincere thanks to the Concept Publishing Company for their acceptance in publishing the book in two volumes.

Gandhigram M. SOUNDARAPANDIAN

CONTENTS

LIST OF CONTRIBUTORS

Anandha Rajakumar, P., Lecturer, Department of Rural Development, Gandhigram Rural Institute, Gandhigram.

Benjamin Christopher, S., Reader, Department of Commerce, Nallamuthu Gounder Mahalingam College (Autonomous), Pollachi.

Choodambigai, S. R., Lecturer (S.G), Department of Economics, Avinashilingam University, Coimbatore.

Gurumoorthy, T. R., Senior Lecturer, Department of International Business and Commerce, Alagappa University, Karaikudi.

Gurunathan, P., Lecturer, Department of Management Studies, PSNA College of Engineering & Technology, Dindigul.

Jagadees Pandi, S., Department of Rural Industries and Management, Gandhigram Rural Institute, Gandhigram.

Jeyachandran, K., Research Scholar, Department of International Business and Commerce, Alagappa University, Karaikudi.

Karthikeyan, M., Director, Space Computer Centre, Gandhigram.

Karunakaran, R., Department of Co-operation, Gandhigram Rural Institute, Gandhigram.

Kokila Devi, L., Lecturer, Department of Economics, K. N. Government Arts College (Women), Thanjavur.

Lalitha, N., Reader in Extension, Gandhigram Rural Institute, Gandhigram.

Madalai Mary, (Mrs.) I., Reader, Department of Economics, K. N. Government Arts College (Women), Thanjavur.

Madhavi, C., Department of Management Studies, D.D.E., Annamalai University, Annamalai Nagar.

Manohar, S. John, Senior Lecturer, Department of Management, Studies, PSNA College of Engineering & Technology, Dindigul.

Meera Mohiadeen, P. M., Lecturer (S.G), Department of Commerce, Jamal Mohamed College, Tiruchirapalli.

Nagarajan, R., Lecturer, Department of Economics, Nallamuthu Gounder Mahalingam College (Autonomous), Pollachi.

Nagarajan, R. N., Department of Co-operation, Gandhigram Rural Institute, Gandhigram.

Nagesh Kumari, N., Lecturer, Department of Economics, P.S.G.R. Krishnammal College for Women, Coimbatore.

Palanivel, S., Department of Rural Industries and Management, Gandhigram Rural Institute, Gandhigram.

Ramasamy, S., Reader, Department of Economics, Gandhigram Rural Institute, Gandhigram.

Rengachari, N. R., Department of International Business and Commerce, Alagappa University, Karaikudi.

Renuka, C., Department of Economics, P.S.G.R. Krishnammal College for Women, Coimbatore.

Samudhara Rajakumar, C., Department of Management Studies, D.D.E., Annamalai University, Annamalai Nagar.

Seethalakshmi, M., Lecturer in Dairying (Sr. Grade), Gandhigram Rural Institute, Gandhigram.

Selvaraj, V. M., Reader, Department of Commerce, A.K.G.S. Arts College, Srivaikuntam.

Shyamala, M., Research Scholar, Department of Economics, Avinashilingam University, Coimbatore.

Siva Kumar, N., Department of Rural Industries and Management, Gandhigram Rural Institute, Gandhigram.

Sivasubramanian, M., Department of Business Administration, D.D.E., Annamalai University, Annamalai Nagar.

Soundarapandian, M., Reader, Department of Rural Industries and Management, Gandhigram Rural Institute, Gandhigram.

Syed Zafar, M., Department of Management Studies, D.D.E., Annamalai University, Annamalai Nagar.

Tharani, N. L., Department of Economics, Gandhigram Rural Institute, Gandhigram.

Thiripurasundari, K., (Mrs.), Department of Commerce, Sri Parasakthi College for Women, Courtallam.

Uma, G., Department of Political Science, Gandhigram Rural Institute, Gandhigram.

Uma Sankar, G., Department of Political Science, Gandhigram Rural Institute, Gandhigram.

1

SMALL SCALE ENTERPRISES : Problems and Prospects

— *S. R.. Choodambigai* and *M. Shyamala*

The Industrial Policy Resolution of 1956, while emphasising the role of Cottage and Small Scale Industries, stated:'They provide immediate large scale employment, they offer a method of ensuring a more equitable distribution of National Income, and they facilitate an effective mobilization of capital and skill, which might otherwise remain unutilized.'

A significant feature of the Indian economy since independence is the rapid growth of the small industry sector, in terms of employment and growth. In spite of the stiff competition from the large sector, and not so encouraging support from the Government, the number of small scale units have grown from 4.2 lakhs in 1973-74 to 23.84 lakhs in 1993-94. During the same period, of 20 years, employment has grown from 4 million to 13.9 million, and output has increased from Rs.7,200 crores to Rs. 241,648 crores (Datt, 1997).

The average annual growth rate of employment in the small scale sector for the period 1980-81 to 1993-94, worked out to be 5.3 per cent, and that of production to be 18.0 per cent.

The growth rate of employment is commendable, but the production figures, conceal the rise in inflation as indicated by Table 1.1.

The annual growth of production of the small sector of 10.9 per cent is much higher than the growth rate of industrial production, in the large sector. Obviously, the growth rate of the small scale sector has been faster, both in terms of output and employment (Datt, 1997).

TABLE 1.1 : Employment and Production in Small Scale Sector

Year	Production (Rs. crores)	Employment (lakhs)	Exports (Rs. crores)
1973-74	7,200	39.7	393
1977-78	14,300	54.0	845
1980-81	28,060	71.0	1,643
1985-86	61,228	96.0	2,769
1987-88	87,300	107.0	4,373
1990-91	1,55,340	125.3	9,100
1991-92	1,78,700	130.0	13,627
1992-93	2,09,300	134.0	17,785
1993-94	2,41,648	139.4	22,764
1994-95	2,93,990	146.56	28,000

Source : All India Report on Functions and Activities (1992-93), Small Industries Development Organisations (SIDO), Department of Small Scale Industry, Government of India, pp.4-16.

It is generally recognised, that the healthy expansion of cottage and small scale industries depends upon a number of factors, like the provision of raw materials, cheap power, technological advancements, and organized marketing of products.

In this connection, we may refer to the problems faced in the production, process of the SSIs, the low capacity utilisation of the small industries, the lack of technical and financial assistance, the availability of raw materials, for the production process and finally the formulation of industrial policy for the small sector.

Wisdom demands that efforts should be made to strengthen the SSI sector, rather than adopting a policy of neglect, or leaving it to the harsh forces of the stifle its growth.

Availability of Raw Materials and Problems in the Production Process

Small enterprises are presently handicapped in comparison with large units by an inequitable allocation system for scarce raw materials and imported components. According to the Report of the International Perspective Planning Team, which studied the problem of availability of raw materials, imported components for production and selected imported equipments to the SSIs, the SSI sector as a whole, has not shared proportionately, the growing supplies of scarce raw materials.[1] In pursuance of this recommendation, the Government started giving priority in raw-material allocation to the small scale sector.

The State Small Industries Development Organization (SSIDO), assists the small scale units in obtaining their raw material requirement, and capital goods for the enterprise. Intervention of the SSIDO, on behalf of the small scale units, in procuring raw materials is helpful and often decisive. In case of certain commodities such as scarce categories of iron and steel items, non-ferrous metals, bulk quotas are allotted to the SSIDO, for distribution to the SSIs.

However, the Seventh Plan, expressed its deep dissatisfaction with SSIDO as "while various measures have been taken for supply of raw materials, to the small scale units, through State Small Industries Development organisations, in actual practice, the sector gets more or less a 'residuary' treatment in raw material distribution/ allocation."[2]

Apart from SSIDO, the NSIC (National Small Industries Corporation) also distributes raw materials to the SSIs on a bulk basis. In village industries, raw materials account for more than 60 per cent of total cost of the product, and in some industries like leather, oil metal products it is even higher — 80 per cent. Only in the paper and palm industry it is 33 per cent.

Table 1.2 indicates the rate of growth of the small scale sector during the Seventh Plan (1985-90). This table reveals that modern small industries sector is more dynamic as compared with the traditional SSIs. In terms of production, the modern sector had a growth rate of 12.4 per cent, as against the traditional sector showing a growth rate of 9.9 per cent. Even in terms of employment and exports, the modern SSI sector outperforms the traditional SSIs. The upshot of the analysis, is that the State has been providing incentives to the modern SSIs whereas the traditional SSI sector, constituting the handlooms and handicrafts, were largely neglected by the Government. They continue to suffer, due to the non-availability of raw materials, for the production process.

TABLE 1.2: Growth Rates of Small Sector during the Seventh Plan

(in percentage)

	Modern	Traditional	Total
Production	12.4	9.9	12.1
Employment	6.1	3.2	4.4
Exports	26.5	26.6	26.6

Source : Draft Eighth Five Year Plan (1992-1997), Planning Commission, Government of India, Vol. 2, p. 133.

On the question of availability of raw materials, which is the major bottleneck in the rapid expansion of small scale units production, the Eighth Plan observes,"In the case of critical raw materials, new enterprises face problems in obtaining these in the absence of a proper and equitable policy of raw material distribution. After the de-control of steel price, drying up of canalising agencies (like MMTC), and the devaluation of the Rupee, the availability of raw materials, particularly to the small producer, has been severely affected."[3]

The solution suggested by the Eighth Plan, to encourage Industry Association, to evolve a suitable distribution mechanism of raw materials, to protect the interests of the small sector, is to say the least, a very undependable solution. It virtually amounts to leaving the allocation pattern, to the dictates of the market. But the market mechanism follows the laws of the jungle, that is "survival of the fittest". It is only with the help or the purposeful intervention of the society, that the survival of the weak or the unfittest SSIs can be ensured.

If civilisation means, the survival of the weak, then the arm of the State must ensure, a policy of equitable distribution of raw materials, but the New Economic Policy, which overbonds in favour of the market mechanism, cannot be trusted to protect the interests of the SSI sector.

Table 1.3 provides information about production of the small sector in India. The data reveals that production of the small sale sector (measured at 1981-82 prices) was of the order of Rs. 14,959 crores in 1973-74, and increased to Rs. 31,212 crores during 1980-81 further shot up to Rs. 85,025 crores in 1990-91, and rose sharply to Rs.1,41,046 crores in 1997-98. Average annual growth of production during the 24 years period was of the order of 10.5 per cent per annum, and it declined, thereafter to 7.5 per cent per annum during 1990-91 to 1997-98. It indicated a fall in the compound growth rate of production in the SSI sector, which is due to the problems in the production processes of the SSIs.

The handicaps of small scale production outweigh the advantages, in most branches of manufacturing activity. As a result, the larger units are generally able to pass on a good part of their advantages in the market place, in the form of lower prices, or better quality of products, giving rise to the small industry problem. In many branches of manufacture, small scale production has disappeared, as exists on the fringe, or is being kept alive by supporting measures.[4] It is true, not only for a large number of small units, in old manufacturing activities — food, textiles and footwear, but also of units in new manufacturing activities — engineering, chemicals and electronic goods.

One of the important problems in the production process is the non-availability of working capital, which tends to interrupt the production process. The proportion of fixed and working capital in a factory is linked to the capital-size of a factory. In tiny units, the proportion of fixed capital is 34.5 per cent, as per Table 1.4, while that of working capital is 65.5 per cent. In small units, the ratio of FC:WC is 49:51, but the trend is reversed in large units where the ratio is 72.28.[5] This underlines the fact that while providing

TABLE 1.3 : Production Process of Small Scale Sector in India

Period	Production of current prices	Price Index (1981-82=100)	Production at 1981-82 prices
1973-74	7,300	48.8	14,959
1980-81	28,060	89.9	31,212
1985-86	61,228	125.4	48,826
1990-91	1,55,340	182.7	85,025
1991-92	1,78,700	207.8	85,996
1992-93	2,09,300	228.7	91,530
1993-94	2,41,648	247.8	97,517
1994-95	2,93,990	274.7	1,07,022
1996-97	4,12,636	314.6	1,33,141
1997-98	4,65,171	329.8	1,41,046

Note : The data at current prices has been converted into 1981-82 prices.
Source : "Report on Currency and Finance", (1998), *Reserve Bank of India Bulletin,* Vol. 2, p. 9.

for capital requirements of SSIs, the State should not confine its role to fixed capital requirements. It is more important to provide working capital needs, so as to maintain the production process smoothly (Dutt, 1999).

TABLE 1.4 : Performance of Small Scale Enterprises (1994-95)
(in percentage)

	Working capital ratio of fixed capital	Fixed Capital per employee	Working capital per employee
Tiny units	34.5	65.5	100
Small units	49.1	50.9	100
Large units	0.40	71.6	92.4

Source : Dutt, R., (1999) "Role of SSEs in Socio-economic Perspective", *Journal of the Indian Association of Social Science,* Vol.18, No.1, pp.8-24.

The production process in the SSIs are greatly affected by lack of proper infrastructural facilities. Lack of water supply, good roads, medical facilities, sanitation, etc. also hamper the production process. Therefore, there is an urgent necessity to address this problem. Production processes in SSIs suffer badly for want of adequate and unfailing supply of power. Frequent power cuts and load shedding have affected the sector badly. In most of the SSIs no qualified technical staff are employed. But one of the major problems faced by the SSIs in the production process is relating to finance. This sector has been facing many constraints in the mobilisation of funds, from different sources, for the last 2 decades due to cyclical fluctuations in the fortunes of the industry.

Non-availability of funds, coupled with raw materials, is one of the major problems of the SSI sector. Moreover low labour productivity, coupled with problems of labour unrest, add to the woes of the SSI units.

If the small sector should move into progress rapidly both in modernisation and diversification of production efforts should be made to improve the level of technology, by producing sophisticated machines within the country.

Technological Problems in the Production Process

In this modern age new technology is making possible decentralised production units, at a high efficiency which at one time seemed impossible. Appropriate technology is not a static, but a dynamic concept, that must change, as the country's technological skills develop. Appropriate technology is primarily meant for SSI's that employ local raw materials, utilise available skills, and cater largely to a local demand.

The general level of technology, in terms of installed equipment, is backward in the SSI sector, when compared to the others. The developments of SSIs is hampered by the present low level of technology, and shortage of trained and experienced technical personnel.

Provision of technical service is an important and justified form of aid, to stimulate increased productive efficiency, and encourage new product lines.

The vast majority of the machines used by the SSI sector are conventional. Moreover, accessories for the imported machines are not manufactured in India. Because of their age, they need constant attention and maintenance, and problem of spare parts is acute. Old machinery, are never replaced due to variety of reasons. Finance, long waiting periods for deliveries, risk aversion are some of the reasons, for the slow replacement of machines in the SSI sector. Those who use indigenous machines generally feel that they lack speed and are made of bad tempered steel, lack precision, lack durability and often lead to frequent repairs. For those who wish to modernise or diversify their production, it is difficult to get imported machines, because of restrictions over imports.[6]

What is needed, right now, is to spot the possibilities, that exist all round, and to either adapt existing techniques or devise new ones for the best utilization of the available raw materials. It is such improvement, effected on a wide scale, that can bring about a revolutionary transformation in the SSI sector.

There are at present two arrangements for providing technical advice and assistance to small firms. First, the Central Small Scale Industries Organization, which, through its Service Institutes provides a staff of technically qualified people, whose job is to give advice to small entrepreneurs on the technical problem facing them, and secondly, the common facility workshops, which undertake production operations, on behalf of the small firms for a cost.[7]

In their glamour for Western techniques, many small entrepreneurs, have neglected and overlooked the tremendous scope for small innovations in the existing practice, which cannot only bring rich dividends to the country as a whole, but also provide help to those who need it most.

The problem in the production process, and technology require a re-examination of the small sector policy, unleashed after the Industrial Policy of 1991, which adversely affected the fortunes of the SSI sector.

Small Sector Industrial Policy

India's Small Industry Policy, has been a widely known phenomena. The relative merits of less capital intensity and more labour absorption capacity among others have endeared the sector to the policy makers as an instrument to achieve a variety of economic objectives such as employment generation, production of mass consumption goods, balanced regional development and equitable distribution of income.

In the pre-reforms era (1947-48 to 1990-91) when Indian economy was subject to controls and regulations, SSIs emphasised protected growth of the sector with a two-pronged strategy, developing institutional network and offering protective benefits. As a consequence, quantitative performance its policy towards the Small Sector, necessitated a change in the direction for small industry policy.[8]

To combat, the emerging competitive environment, redefining the SSI policy became imperative. The New Industrial Policy Introduced in August 1991, marked the beginning of economic reforms in India. The main features of the policy are:

The Small Sector has emerged as a dynamic and vibrant sector of the economy during the 80s. At the end of the Seventh Plan period, it accounted for nearly 35 per cent of the gross value of output in the manufacturing sector and over 40 per cent of the total exports from the country. It also provided employment opportunities to around 12 million people.

The primary objective of SSI policy during the 90s was to impart more vitality and growth impetus to the Sector, to enable it to contribute its fullest to the economy, particularly in terms of growth of output, employment and exports.[9]

A new ministry has been formed at the Centre to cater to the needs of the small sector. The Small Industry Policy is quite ambivalent in India. The United Front Government in 1997, raised the investment limits in SSIs from Rs. 60 lakh to Rs. 3 crores. Now the present NDA Government has brought it down to Rs.1 crore. The UF Government rationalised it on the grounds of imperatives of growth and technology upgradation. The present Government says it wants to genuinely support the small units. What this policy change under scores is that the SSI category vastly subsumes different types of units with very different, even conflicting interest.[10]

The New Industrial Policy comprised the elimination of all

entry barriers, to most industries as well as the associated constraints on scale and technology. Industrial liberlisation was complemented by trade liberlisation on scale and technology. Industrial liberlisation was complemented by trade liberalisation in the form of drastic reduction in customs duties and removal of restrictions on imports of raw materials, intermediates and capital goods.

Apparently the policy does not signify any major deviation from the past. But a minute perusal does indicate that the policy intends to promote competitiveness of the sector, more than anything else. Unlike in the past, the policy does not contain, mere intentions of the Government, it has proposed clear for the Sector- 1. Finance, 2. Marketing, 3. Technology, as indicated by Table 1.5.

TABLE 1.5 : Essential Features of the SSI Policy : 1991

Sl. No.	Objectives	Major features
1.	To meet the emerging demand for credit	Emphasis to shift from cheap credit to adequate credit
		Equity participation by other undertakings, domestic, foreign upto 24 per cent
2.	To strengthen small industry marketing	Introduction of factoring services through Banks
		Marketing of mass consumption goods under common brand name
		Setting up subcontracting exchanges
3.	To upgrade technology and promote modernisation	Technology development cell in SIDO
		Quality counselling and testing technology information centres
		Technology upgradation programmes

Source : SIDO Report on Functions and Activities, (1992-93), "Policy measures for promoting and strengthening small, tiny and village Industries", Department of Small Industry, Government of India, pp. 4-16.

The problems of SSI's in these areas are closely linked. It is due to insufficient quality, the SSI's face the problem of marketing. To improve quality, many of these require to go for technology upgradation and modernisation. The New Policy has attempted to address these problems.[11]

What is significant, is that the policy carved out greater scope for the involvement of State governments and particularly Industry Associations. All these emphasized that the SSI policy in the 90s will be on competitive growth rather than on protected growth.

From Table 1.6, it appears that the Government is evolving a focused approach for SSI development in the 90s which has 3 dimensions:

TABLE 1.6 : New Policy Initiatives for SSIs in 1990:Major Areas

Sl. No.	Technology	Finance	Marketing
1.	Technology Bureau to be set up by SIDBI	Factoring services by SIDBI and PSBs	Setting up of subcontracting exchanges
2.	Quality counselling centres to be set up	SIDBI branches in SSI clusters	Access to international exhibitions by SIDBI, NSIC
3.	Exhibitions for technology purchase	Exclusive bank branches in SSI	Credit rating arrangements districts
4.	Technology development and modernisation fund to be set up	National equity fund for SSIs	SIDO to support export promotion
5.	Collaborative technology upgradation programmes by SBI	Financial support acquire ISO - 9000 Certificate	EDP programmes to be arranged

Source : Balasubramanya, M.H., (2000), "India's Small Industry Policy in the 90s - waning protectionism", *The Indian Economic Journal*, Vol.47, No. 2, pp.76-79.

1. The development of SSIs are vast and varied. To evolve an effective approach, it is necessary to concentrate on major of concern.
2. The SSIs are widely scattered. So cluster-based policy initiatives are to be evolved.
3. To have an effective implementation, the involvement of the sector itself is crucial.

The test of the performance of the Government, should be to the extent to and effectiveness with which, it performs the role of an arbiter. If this be the criteria, the Government should be evaluated in terms of their political commitment to the small sector. The question therefore how much transparent is the SSI sector, in the realm of planning and administration.

Therefore, in this context, the SSI policy needs to clarify: 1. Policy Perception, 2. Reservation, 3. Role of the Government, 4. Centre-State Relations, 5. Technology and Competitiveness and 6. Legal Framework.

The SSI Policy — A Critical Outlook

The policy perception on the role and relevance of the SSI sector has not undergone any radical changes since independence. While the Nehruvian emphasis under the Mahalanobis Models gave way to the target group oriented approaches during the subsequent decades, and finally to the liberalisation paradigm since 1991, there have been few quantitative changes in policy. The talk about Panchayat Raj, Decentralisation, Strengthening Co-operatives, liberation from Inspector Raj, etc. are common usages that appear in most plan documents, irrespective of the Party in Power.[12]

Regarding the SSIs we are still living in the Nehruvian era. Small industry development, be it in the Centre or in the States, is still a classic case of patronage and exploitation. The SSIs have a lot to offer in the generation of employment opportunities. But here again the Government fails to perform its supporting role. Decentralization has been offered as a solution. But it may not work without transparency and accountability in the system. The last two Union Budgets had only taken cosmetic steps like earmarking a few crores of rupees to the corpus of specialised development banks like NABARD, SIDBI, and setting up a few SSI branches of commercial banks. Banks are asked to lend more to this sector, which usually does not happen.

The good intentions of the Policy Statement of 1991, did not translate into results. The Abid Hussein Committee, which was appointed by the Ministry of Industry, made some recommendations in this area, for total de-reservation of the SSI sector and opening it to competition. However the issue remains divided.[13]

A study of SSIs by the Confederation of Indian Industry in 1999 has been reported as having brought out that close to one-half of the 450 enterprises studied, felt that their growth was bogged down, because of the Government's regulatory practices and policies.

In the wake of the policy of deregulation, big units in the organized sector have been reaping benefits meant for the small sector.

If the SSIs are to row further, and make much more significant contribution in our National Economy, then the Government must remove the lacunae of laws governing the reservation policy. The Centre must not buckle under pressure from WTO.

What we need right now is a national policy on the small scale sector, and also a perspective plan which could be integrated into the planning process. We need a triangle of enterprise development, the vertices being transparency, accountability and information. Irrespective of the Government support, it is the vulnerability to the international market that is going to shape the future of the Indian SSIs.[14]

Conclusion

Under the policy measures for promoting and strengthening SSIs and tiny industries, it has been enunciated that adequate and equitable distribution of raw materials, problem-free production processes, advanced technology and infrastructural facilities, would be ensured to small sector. Thus there is a significant change in the overall strategy for a SSI development. It may be too early to judge the sufficiency of the strategy to bring out the desired outcome. But internationally rapid technological changes are revitalising the SSIs and it is perceived that future role of SSIs will be based on competition, productivity and efficiency. In this context, the shifting policy emphasis in India is a welcome change.

Notes and References

1. Datt, R. and Sundara, M.K.P.M. (1997), *Indian Economy,* S. Chand and Co. Publishers, New Delhi, pp. 611-626.
2. Datt, R. (1999), "Role of SSEs in socio-economic perspective", *Journal of the Indian Association of Social Science,* Vol.18, No.1, pp. 8-24.
3. Balasubramanya, M.H. (2000), "India's Small Industry Policy in the 90s - waning protectionism", *The Indian Economic Journal,* Vol. 47, No. 2, p. 76.
4. Subramanya, S. (2000), "Doing without Reservation in the small sector", *The Southern Economist,* Vol. 39, No. 10, pp. 1-3.
5. Adikari, C.S. (2000), "Enterprise Development for Rural Employment — A Project Report", *Economic and Political Weekly,* Vol. 35, No. 20, pp. 1858-1864.
6. Goldar, B. (2000) "Employment Growth in Organised Manufacturing in India", *Economic and Political Weekly,* Vol. 35, No. 14, pp. 1191-1997.
7. Chaudhri, S. (2000), "Small Industries — Round the Mulberry Bush", *Economic and Political Weekly,* Vol. 35, No. 1, p. 4.
8. Mathew, P.M. (2000), "Small Industries — Problems of Policy", *Economic and Political Weekly,* No. 17 pp. 1320-1324.
9. Giri, V.V. (1975), *Small Industries in the Seventies,* Vikas Publications, London, pp.175-193.
10. Khandelwal, N.M. (1985), *Working Capital Management in SSIs,* Ashish Publishing Co., New Delhi, pp. 45-65.
11. SIDO Report on Functions and Activities, (1992-93), "Policy Measures for promoting and strengthening small, tiny all village industries", Department of SSI, Government of India, pp. 4-16.
12. The Draft Eighth Five Year Plan Report, (1992-97), Planning Commission, Government of India, Vol. 2, p. 133.
13. *The Reserve Bank of India Bulletin,* (1998), "Report on Currency and Finance", Vol. 2, p. 9.
14. The Draft Seventh Five Year Plan Report (1985-1990), Planning Commission, Government of India, Vol. 2, p. 102.

2

PROGRESS OF SMALL SCALE INDUSTRY : A Study

— *T.R. Gurumoorthy* and *K. Jeyachandran*

Introduction

Small Scale Industry accelerates Indian economy not only in terms of its contribution to industrial output and national export but also in growing employment opportunities. Small Scale Industry accounts for about 95 per cent of industrial units, contributes about 40 per cent of the value added manufacturing sector and over 33 per cent of the national exports through 28 lakh units spread all over the country.

Meaning of Small Scale Industries

The Government of India grouped Small Scale Industrial undertakings into two categories — those using power but employing less than 50 persons and those not using power but employing less than 100 persons. All small scale enterprises, however had capital investment of less than Rs. 5 lakhs. The ownership and management in small enterprises is predominantly proprietary with individual ownership or partnership.

As per the Industrial Policy Statement of May 1990, the investment ceiling in plant and machinery for small scale industries (fixed in 1985) has been raised from Rs. 35 lakhs to Rs. 60 lakhs and correspondingly for ancillary units from Rs. 45 lakhs to 75 lakhs. Investment ceiling with respect to tiny units has been increased from Rs. 2 lakhs to Rs. 5 lakhs. According to the modified definition an ancillary unit is one which sells not less than 50 per cent of its manufactures to one or more industrial units.

During 1997, on the recommendation of Abid Hussain Committee, the Government has raised the investment limit on plant and machinery for small units and ancillaries from Rs. 60.75 lakhs to Rs. 3 crores and that for tiny units from Rs. 5 lakhs to Rs. 25 lakhs. As per the new policy initiatives in 1999-2000 (for the small scale sector) the investment limit for small scale and ancillary undertakings has been reduced from existing Rs. 3 crores to Rs. 1 crore.

The important objectives of this study are given below :

(i) To study the progress of small scale industry in terms of production, employment and exports;

(ii) To study the new policy initiatives announced in 1999-2000 for the small scale sector;

(iii) To compare the sick units in SSI sector with sick units in non-SSI sector in terms of number of sick units and amount outstanding;

(iv) To analyze financial assistance provided by the commercial banks to SSI sector; and

(v) To review the reason for the sickness in SSI sector.

The present study is descriptive and analytical and it is based on secondary data. Report on Currency and Finance, Reserve Bank of India, Economic Survey, Government of India, *Laghu Udyog Samachar* (News Magazine on Small Scale Industries), Books, research papers, journals and periodicals relating to small scale sector are important sources of secondary data of this study. Discussion with academicians, researchers, industrialists and officials of the SSI sector is also done for ascertaining the progress of small scale industry and its pressing problems.

Progress of Small Scale Industry

Progress of small scale industry is analyzed in this study in terms of number of units, production, employment and exports. Target *Vs.* Achievement analysis is also done to study the progress of SSI sector. Table 2.1 shows progress of small scale industry for the period 1996-97 to 1998-99.

TABLE 2.1 : Progress of Small Scale Industry

Year	No. of Units in lakhs	Production (Rs. in cr)		Employment (Rs. in cr)		Exports (Rs.in cr)		% of Export in Production
		T	A	T	A	T	A	
1996-97	28.57	385454	412636	158.91	160.00	20207	39247	9.5
			(-)	(-)	(-)	(-)	(-)	
1997-98	30.14	440098	465171	166.86	167.00	47905	44437	9.5
	(5)		(13)		(4)	(-)	(13)	
1998-99	31.21	508906	538357	175.20	172.58	57488	49481	9.19
	(9)		(30)		(7)	(-)	(26)	

T - Target A - Actual
Source : Report on Currency and Finance, 1998-99, Reserve Bank of India.

Table 2.1 reveals that number of SSI units is increased from 28.57 lakhs in 1996-97 to 31.21 lakhs units in 1998-99, recording the percentage increase of 9 per cent.

Production of SSI sector was at Rs. 412636 crore in 1996-97 and it increased to Rs. 538357 crore in 1998-99 registering the percentage increase of 30 per cent.

The SSI sector employment during the period 1996-97 was at

160 lakhs and raised to 171.58 lakhs in 1998-99 and the percentage increase of employment during the period 1996-97 to 1998-99 is 7 per cent.

Exports of the SSI sector is increased from Rs. 39247 crore in 1996-97 to Rs. 49481 crore in 1998-99 showing the percentage increase of 26 per cent.

Exports of the SSI sector in its total production is 9.5 per cent in 1996-97 and 1997-98 and it is decreased to 9.1 per cent in 1998-99.

Target Vs. Achievement Analysis

Targets for Production, employment and exports are compared with achievements to analyze progress of SSI sector during the period 1996-97 to 1998-99. Table 2.2 shows target and achievement in small scale industry.

TABLE 2.2 : Target *Vs.* Achievement Analysis

Year	% of Achievement over target		
	Production	Employment	Exports
1996-97	107.03	100.69	194.23
1997-98	105.68	100.08	92.75
1998-99	105.73	97.93	86.07

Source : Annual, 1998-99, Ministry of Industry, Government of India.

Table 2.2 shows that during the period 1996-97 to 1998-99 actual production in small scale sector is more than the targeted production. The percentage of actual production over the target are 107.03 per cent in 1996-97, 105.68 per cent in 1997-98 and 105.73 per cent to 1998-99.

Actual employment created by SSI sector is marginally increased over the target during the period 1996-97 to 1998-99 and in the year 1998-99 actual employment generated is less than the target.

Export in SSI sector crossed the target in 1996-97. The

percentage of actual export over the target in 1996-97 is 194.23 per cent. Later actual export is less than the target. It is 92.75 per cent in 1997-98 and 86.07 per cent in 1998-99. Increasing competition in the international market is a basic reason for this decrease in export over the target in SSI sector.

New Policy Initiatives for SSI Sector

* Announcement of a new Credit Insurance Scheme in the Budget (1999-2000) for providing adequate security to banks and improving flow of investment credit to SSI units, particularly export oriented and tiny units.
* The working capital limit for SSI units is determined by the banks on the basis of 20 per cent of their annual turnover. The turnover limit for this purpose has been enhanced from Rs. 4 crore to Rs. 5 crore.
* To increase the reach of banks to the tiny sector, lending by banks to non-banking financial companies (NBFCs) or other financial intermediaries for purposes of non-lending to the tiny sector, has been included within the definition of priority sector for bank lending.
* Excise exemption is increased from Rs. 50 lakhs to Rs. 1 crore.
* Exemption from excise duty, as given to SSI units, will be extended to goods bearing a brand name of another manufacturer in rural areas.
* A National programme for rural industrialisation has been announced, with a mission to set up 100 rural clusters every year.
* To coordinate the latest development with regard to the World Trade Organization (WTO), a cell has been set up in the office of DC (SSI) to disseminate information to SSI Associations and SME units, regarding recent developments, prepare policies for SSIs in tune with the WTO agreements and organizing WTO sensitization seminars, workshops.
* Cotton yarn has been included in the general excise exemption scheme for SSIs.

* Small job workers, engaged in printing of glazed tiles, have been exempted from excise duty.
* The investment limit for small scale and ancillary undertakings has been reduced from existing Rs. 3 crore to Rs. 1 crore.

Sickness in SSI Sector

Sickness is SSI sector and non-SSI sector is analyzed for the purpose of ascertaining the number of sick units and volume of loan outstanding in both sectors. A small scale industrial unit is considered as sick when, (i) any of its borrowal accounts has become a doubtful advance, i.e. principal or interest in respect of any of its borrowed accounts has remained overdue for a period exceeding 2-½ years and (ii) there is erosion in the net worth due to accumulated cash losses to the extent of 50 per cent or more of its peak net worth during the preceding two accounting years.

A non-SSI industrial unit is defined as a 'weak' unit, if its accumulated losses as at the end of any accounting year resulted in the erosion of 50 per cent or more of its peak net worth in the immediately preceding four accounting years. It is clarified that weak unit will not include those units which fall within the purview of Sick Industrial Companies (Special Provision) Act, 1985, (viz. Industrial Companies) but also other categories such as partnership firms, proprietary concerns, etc. A 'weak' industrial company would be termed as a potential 'sick' company if and when it is reported to BIFR in terms of section 23(1) of SICA, 1985 amended upto February, 1994.

Table 2.3 reveals number of sick units and volume of loan outstanding in SSI sector and non-SSI sector during the year 1997 and 1998.

Table 2.3 highlights sickness in SSI sector in the years 1997 and 1998. Number of SSI sick units in India were 2,35,032 in 1997. Out of the total SSI units, 45 per cent units were in East India, 16 per cent units in West India, 21 per cent units in North India and 18 per cent units in South India.

TABLE 2.3 : Sickness in SSI Sector in 1997

Region	Sick Units	1997 SSI Sector		Sick Units	1998 SSI Sector	
		Loan Out-standing Rs. in Cr.	Loan Out-standing/ Unit Rs. in Cr.		Loan Out-standing Rs. in Cr.	Loan Out-standing/ Unit Rs. in Cr.
East India	105109 (45)	627 (17)	0.05	106756 (48)	649 (17)	0.60
West India	38549 (16)	1129 (31)	2.92	33758 (15)	1138 (30)	3.37
North India	49964 (21)	850 (24)	1.70	40579 (18)	995 (25)	2.35
South India	41407 (18)	1003 (28)	2.42	40443 (19)	1115 (28)	2.76
Total	235029 (100)	3609 (100)	1.50	221536 (100)	3897 (100)	1.74
Sickness in Non-SSI Sector						
East India	423 (18)	1754 (17)	4.15	419 (17)	1880 (16)	4.48
West India	742 (31)	2912 (29)	3.92	767 (31)	3563 (30)	4.65
North India	511 (22)	2037 (20)	3.98	526 (21)	2472 (21)	4.70
South India	692 (29)	3474 (34)	5.02	764 (31)	3910 (33)	5.11
Total	2368 (100)	10178 (100)	4.30	2476 (100)	11825 (100)	4.78

Majority of the SSI sick units were situated in East India in 1997. The same trend was prevailed in 1998 also.

Total loan outstanding in SSI sick units in 1997 was at Rs. 3609 crore. In it the share of sick units in East India was 17 per cent, West India 31 per cent, North India 24 per cent and South India 18 per cent.

Loan outstanding per sick unit in 1997 in East India was Rs. 0.50 lakh, in West India Rs. 2.92 lakhs, North India Rs. 1.70 lakhs and in South India Rs. 2.42 lakhs.

In 1998 loan outstanding per sick unit was Rs. 0.60 lakh in East India, in West India Rs. 3.37 lakhs, in North India Rs. 2.35 lakhs and in South India Rs. 2.76 lakhs.

It may be concluded that loan outstanding per sick unit in West India is more than the other parts of the country. Number of sick units in East India is higher than the other parts of the country.

Sick units in Non-SSI Sector were at 2368 and 2476 in 1997 and 1998 respectively. Loan outstanding in sick units in Non-SSI sector is more than the sick units in SSI sector. In 1997 loan outstanding per sick unit in Non-SSI sector was at Rs. 4.30 crore, whereas in SSI sector it was Rs. 1.50 lakhs. In 1998 loan outstanding per sick unit in Non-SSI sector was at Rs. 4.78 crore, whereas in SSI sector it is Rs. 1.74 lakhs.

It may be concluded that sick units loan outstanding and loan outstanding per sick unit in Non-SSI sector are higher than the SSI sector. It indirectly reveals that SSI sector is not adequately financed by the Commercial Banks. Number of sick units and loan outstanding in Non-SSI sector in South India were more than the other parts of the country in 1997.

Financial Assistance

Timely availability of finance is one of the requisites for the success of the small scale industry. In order to ensure timely availability of finance to SSI and tiny sector, the Reserve Bank of India has given direction to the commercial banks that out of the funds normally available for the SSI sector, 40 per cent be given to units with investment in plant and machinery upto Rs. 5 lakhs, 20 per cent to units with investment between Rs. 5 lakhs and Rs. 25 lakhs and remaining 40 per cent for other units. Commercial banks have been instructed to establish a large number of specialized SSI branches.

The Economic Survey, Government of India, reveals that "the State of tiny sector in the advances to SSI sector has decreased from 27 per cent at the end of March 1998 to 20.7 per cent at the end of March 1999. Thus, against the target of 60 per cent of SSI credit to tiny units, actual flow at 20.7 per cent, is very low." The Nayak Committee (1991-92) recommended that commercial banks should provide working capital loan to SSI sector equivalent to 20 per cent of its value of production. Table 2.4 reveals financial assistance provided by the commercial banks to the SSI sector during the period 1972 to 1999.

The Abid Hussain Committee recommended that commercial banks should earmark 70 per cent of priority sector lending allocated to small scale sector to the tiny sector. This Committee has suggested that the threshold investment units for SSI units should be Rs. 3 crore and SSI reservation should be withdrawn.

TABLE 2.4 : Financial Assistance to SSI Sector

Year	Financial Assistance to SSI Sector Rs. in Cr.	Gross Bank Credit Rs.in Cr.	% of SSI Credit in Gross Bank Credit
1972	597	548	11
1975	1043	8786	12
1980	2635	21235	12
1985	6612	47956	14
1990	15615	102783	15
1994	22620	156836	14
1996	31884	231860	14
1998	43508	300283	14
1999	48483	342012	14

Source : Report on Trend and Progress of Banking in India, Various Issues, Reserve Bank of India.

Table 2.4 reveals that SSI sector is not adequately financed by the commercial banks. SSI credit to Gross bank credit during the period 1980 to 1999 is 12 to 15 per cent. In total gross bank credit only 14 per cent was provided to SSI sector from the period 1994 to 1999.

During the period 1996-97 to 1998-99, production in SSI sector is increased by 30 per cent, whereas SSI credit to gross bank credit during this period remains at 14 per cent. It shows that recommendations of Abid Hussain Committee and Nayak Committee are not properly implemented in commercial banks in providing credit to SSI sector.

Annual Survey of Industries 1994-95 states that the value added per unit of capital in tiny units (upto Rs. 5 lakhs) is 0.78, Small Scale units (upto Rs. 50 lakhs) 0.61 and in large scale units it is 0.27. Value added per unit of capital employed in tiny sector is higher than the other sectors. Considering this special features commercial banks should come forward to extend financial assistance liberally to tiny and small scale units.

Reasons for Sickness in SSI Sector

Financial and marketing problems are inherent in SSI sector, Professors Rudder Datt and Sundaram in their book, *Small Scale Enterprises* has stated that "Nearly 50 per cent of the closures of SSI units were either the result of scarcity of working capital or their inability to market their products." Specific problems of the SSI sector are highlighted in the Report of the Second All India Census of Small Scale Industries Units (1992). In this report 'Financial problem' is stated as the reason for closure of 35 per cent of the units. This is more or less applicable in every industry. In case of 19.4 per cent of units 'marketing problems' is stated as the reasons for closure. Here also, between industries, there is no much of a change in pattern. 'Non-availability of raw material' is stated as the reason for closure by 5.6 per cent of units 2.2 per cent are stated to be closed down due to labour problems. While 19 per cent reported to have closed for other reasons. It may be concluded that financial problem, marketing problem and raw material problems are important problems of the SSI units.

Foreign trade policy is also a potential threat to SSI sector. On the other side it may be considered as opportunity also to upgrade the SSI sector at par with the 14 multinationals.

Removal of Quantitative Restrictions (OR) for the 714 items in the recent EXIM policy is a threat to SSI sector. Multinationals' products will compete with the SSI products in Indian market. Company may be multinational. But products will be Indianised and relevant to Indian market exclusively. Unless SSI sector strengthens its all factors of production, technology and facilitating functions, the progress of the SSI sector will be a day dream in the days to come. The SSI sector is unable to manufacture internationally competitive products in sectors like sports goods, leather footwear and readymade garments.

Suggestions of Confederation of Indian Industry

CII has suggested a 10-point agenda for the SMEs .

* Linkage of priority sector lending target for banks with incremental deposits instead of bank advances;
* Need to encourage bills culture to mitigate delayed payments;
* Establishment of a small industry technology development fund with SIDBI;
* Establishment of Single Small Business Establishment Act;
* Enactment of Securitisation Act for SSIs;
* Enactment of utility model law for providing a second tier protection;
* Review the existing export clusters and upgrade their infrastructural facilities;
* The quantum of deduction (section 801B) for a newly established SSI unit be enhanced to 40 per cent of profit from the present 25 per cent;
* A three-tier custom duty structure;
* Reduce special excise on select items.

Announcements made by the Finance Minister for The SSI Sector

The key announcements made by the Finance Minister for the SSI sector, during Union Budget 2000-2001 :

* Increase the limit of collateral free loans for the tiny sector from Rs. 1 lakh to Rs. 5 lakh;
* Composite loan limit for the Small Industries Development Bank of India (SIDBI) and banks for small borrowers increased from Rs. 5 lakh to Rs.10 lakh;
* Dedicated bank branches having ISO certification to serve every district and SSI cluster;
* Rs. 100 crore provided to the Credit Guarantee Scheme for SSIs, through SIDBI, to cover loans up to Rs. 10 lakhs from the banking sector;
* Project limit under SIDBI's National Equity Fund Scheme raised from Rs. 15 lakh to Rs. 25 lakh;
* SIDBI scheme of Technology Development and Modernization Fund Scheme extended for another 3 years.
* Khadi and Village Industries Commission (KVIC) to introduce a common brand name for its products and set up a professionally managed marketing company. These were supplemented by the announcements made by Prime Minister Atal Behari Vajpayee in August 2000;
* Increase in the Excise exemption limit to Rs. 1 crore from Rs. 50 lakh;
* Enhancement in the limit for composite loans from Rs. 10 lakh to Rs. 25 lakh; entrepreneurs will now be able to secure term loans and working capital from the same agency;
* Industry related service and business enterprises with a maximum investment of Rs. 10 lakh will qualify for priority lending;
* Capital subsidy of 12 per cent for investment in technology in select sectors;
* Setting up of a group to recommend, within three months, means of streamlining inspections. These would include repeal of laws and regulations applicable to the sector, that have since

become redundant;

* Fresh census of SSIs to cover, *inter alia,* the incidence of sickness and its causes;
* Extension of reimbursement scheme to the extent of Rs.75,000 for the next six years, for the SSI units opting for ISO 9000 certification;
* One time capital grant of 50 per cent to small scale associations, who wish to develop and operate testing laboratories, provided they are of international standard.

Findings of the Study

The important findings of the study are given below :

(i) Number of units in SSI sector is increased from 28.57 lakhs units in 1996-97 to 31.21 lakhs units in 1998-99.

(ii) The percentage increase in production in SSI sector during the period 1996-97 to 1998-99 is 30 per cent, employment generation 7 per cent and growth in export 26 per cent.

(iii) 9.5 per cent of SSI production is exported to foreign country.

(iv) Actual production in SSI sector during the period 1996-97 to 1998-99 is more than the targeted production, whereas in employment and export actual performance is less than the target in 1997-98 and 1998-99.

(v) Threshold limit to SSI sector for investment is reduced from Rs. 3 crore to Rs. 1 crore. This policy may not be helpful to SSI sector. The emerging competition is to modernize itself. Technology upgradation becomes necessary in SSI sector. Excise concession may not be the right motivator to SSI sector.

(vi) A large number of SSI sick units are situated in East India. Total loan outstanding in sick SSI unit and loan per unit in West India is more than the other parts of the country. Loan outstanding in sick SSI units is increased from Rs. 3609 crore in 1997 to Rs. 3867 crore in 1998.

(vii) Loan outstanding in sick SSI units in Non-SSI sector is increased from Rs. 10,171 crore 1997 to Rs. 11,825 crore in 1998. Loan outstanding in sick units in Non-SSI sector is more than the SSI sector.

(viii) Loan outstanding per sick unit in Non-SSI sector is Rs. 4.30 crore in 1997 and Rs. 4.78 crore in 1998.

(ix) Loan outstanding per sick unit in Non-SSI sector in South India is more than the other parts of the country.

(x) SSI credit to gross bank credit remains at 14 per cent during the period 1994 to 1999.

(xi) Finance problem, marketing problem and non-availability of raw materials are basic reasons for sickness in SSI units.

References

A Hand Book for Entrepreneurs, Small Industries Service Institute, Madras, 1992.

Desai, Vasant, *Management of Small Scale Industries,* Himalaya Publishing House, Bombay, 1989.

Economic Survey, 1999-2000.

"Entrepreneurship and Small Scale Industry", *Economic Times,* September 9, 1990.

Gangadhara Rao, N., *Entrepreneurship and Growth of Enterprise in Industrial Estates,* Deep and Deep Publications, New Delhi, 1986.

Gupta, C.B. and Srinivasan, N. P., *Entrepreneurial Development,* Sultan Chand and Sons, New Delhi, 1992.

"Industry", *Tamilnadu — An Economic Appraisal 1996-97,* pp. 91-130.

Jain, O.P., *Small Industry Exports,* S. Chand & Co., (Pvt.) Ltd., New Delhi, 1971.

Jain, R.K., The Small Scale Industry proved a Mixed Blessing in India, *Southern Economist,* June 15, 1990.

Khan, R.R., *Management of Small Scale Industries,* S.Chand and Co., Ltd., New Delhi.

Mehla, H.S., *Industrial Growth and Regional Development of India,* Print Well Publishers, Jaipur, 1989.

Pattanaik, S.M., *Development Strategy for Small Industries,* Himalaya Publishing House, Bombay, 1988.

R.B.I Credit Policy and Industrial Development, *Pangu Market,* 8-14, November, 1993.

Report Currency and Finance 1998-99, R.B.I. IV-1 to IV-28.

"Role of Small Scale Industries in Export Trade", *HRD Times,* Vol. 2, No. 8 August, 2000.

Sivaprakasam, D., Entrepreneurial Development in Small Scale Industrial Units in Pasumpon Muthuramalinga Thevar District. Ph.D.Thesis submitted to Alagappa University, Karaikudi, June 1993.

Small Industry, *Tamil Nadu Small Scale Industries Association,* September, 1991, Madras.

"Small Scale Industry and its Development", *Valarthozhil,* November 10, 1990.

Subbi Reddy, T. and Apparao, P.B., *Sickness in Small Industry,* Himalaya Publishing House, Bombay, 1980.

3

PROBLEMS OF RURAL INDUSTRIES INCLUDING COTTAGE AND SMALL SCALE INDUSTRIES

— *S. John Manohar* and *P. Gurunathan*

Preamble

In a vast country like India with an area of 32.76 lakh sq.kms and about 80 per cent of the population living in 5,68,000 villages, the entire demand potential of rural market is the major market for all the consumer goods as well as industrial goods for the rural industries of the marketeers of these products. Production as well as marketing functions are becoming increasingly scientific and technical leading to specialisation and professionalism. Changes have taken place in quality and magnitude, in processes and practices and designs and patterns, small scale and cottage industries can ill-afford to be oblivious of this factor.

In fifties and sixties, the phenomenal growth in Rural Industries has, by and large, been the result of restriction on imports and deliberate policy of encouraging import substitution. This provided a vast field to Rural Industries including cottage and small scale industries to operate and fill up the gap created by import restrictions. On account of these factors the need for effective and scientific management was seldom felt by these industries.

However, the recent developments indicate that these favourable conditions do not exist anymore and therefore management of Rural industries has become a problem to reckon with. Hence, a study on Problems of Rural Industries with reference to Raw materials, Inventory, Production Process etc., was undertaken by the authors which is discussed in detail in this chapter.

Profile of the Study

The existing and the emergence of entrepreneurs would promote growth in industrial development, bring out socio-economic reform, ensure better standards of living and ultimately increase the status in the society. Of late, there has been entrepreneurial wave as a result of the efforts by the Government to increase self-employment for unemployed technocrats and other unemployed skilled persons. Moreoftenthannot it is observed that their choice of line of business is based not only on market analysis and potential profitability, but only on the basis of other's followings. This attitude of the enthusiastic entrepreneurs coupled with other infrastructural problems result in closer of the units at one time or other. In order to identify the problems faced by these types of industries mainly located in rural areas and also manufacturing units producing goods for rural market, a detailed study was undertaken among the rural industries in and around Dindigul town.

Objectives of the Study

The researchers have identified the following as the objectives of the study pertaining to Rural Industries in rural including small scale and cottage industries :

(a) To study the nature and extent of problems with respect to availability and sources of raw materials,
(b) Problems with respect to technological and financial aspects of the Rural Industries,
(c) Problems with respect to Government Policies in areas like sales tax, excise duty etc.,
(d) Problems with respect to marketing of products in terms of

package, pricing, storage, selling, distribution, transport and marketing information, and

(e) Problems of nature other than above specified ones.

Scope and Limitations

The study conducted is limited in scope and covers 30 small scale industries and 30 cottage industries falling under the purview of Rural industries as defined above, located in and around Dindigul town.

Methodology

The study was conducted with 60 randomly selected Rural Industries, the list of which was obtained from District Industries Centre and Dindigul Cottage Association covering a wide range of products like coir, agarbathis, candles, etc., in cottage industry sector and fertilizer mixing, textile weaving, candles etc., in small scale industry sector. An interview schedule with a check list was used for interviews with sample units to collect data. Data collection and interviews were carried out by the authors themselves and all the findings reported here are based on them only.

Results : Problems of Rural Industries

The rural industries including small and cottage industries have been facing problems of varied nature which can be broadly categorized into (i) Internal and (ii) External. A detailed list of problems highlighted by them are given in Table 3.1.

Industry Profile

The profile of the Rural industries in the sample size are as follows:

Socio-economic Profile

The existence profile of the industries revealed that 40 per cent have been in the line of business either manufacturing and marketing or marketing only for more than 5 years and the remaining for less than 5 years. The educational profile of the main persons carrying on the business revealed that 46 per cent had collegiate education, 86 per cent were married, 60 per cent had monthly income below Rs. 7500.00 and 60 per cent belonged to nuclear families.

The study revealed that 67 percentage of the units carried out of the business in rental building, 69 per cent entered into the line of business without any prior experience, 30 per cent only had undergone training and 96 per cent had the line of business as their own. Regarding Time Management 87 per cent were of the view that they were not able to fully devote their time on manufacturing only thereby not able to concentrate on the quality of the product.

TABLE 3.1 : Problems faced by Rural Industries

Internal	*External*
• Ideation and choice of an idea	• Infrastructure
• Planning with flaws.	(a) Location of the unit
• Poor project implementation	(b) Power
• Mismanagement/Poor Management	(c) Water
• Less production	(d) Communication
• Lack of Marketing	• Financial
• Inadequate finance	(a) Capital/Working capital
• Labour problems	• Raw material
• Lack of Training	• Marketing
• Lack of strategies	• Tax and other such levies
	• Technology
	• Competition

The information on the individuals running the Units and information on Industry surveyed are depicted in Table 3.2 and Table 3.3.

Constraints Faced : Self-sphere System Constraints

Among the constraints faced by the individuals of the Rural industries, lack of leisure time (0.89 mean score) scored the highest rank. 64 per cent had lack of knowledge about the various assistants

TABLE 3.2 : Information on Individuals

Education	Formal 26 Nos.	Informal 32 Nos.
Marital Status	Married 50 Nos.	Unmarried 8 Nos.
Family Size	Nuclear 34 Nos.	Large 24 Nos.
Monthly Income	< Rs. 7500 34 Nos.	> Rs. 7500 24 Nos.

TABLE 3.3 : Information on Industries Surveyed

Existence	Above 5 years 24 units	Less than 5 years 36 units
Category	CI 30 units	SSI 30 units
Form	Proprietorship 58	Partnership 2
Building	Rental 40	Own 20
Prior Experience	Yes 18	No 42
Training	Yes 18	No 42

and procedures of financial institutions which were the main constraints. Excessive work load due to lack of proper infrastructure and pressure on meeting the delivery schedule were again the constraints highlighted.

Socio-psycho System Constraints

Very less number of persons had any problem with regard to status in the society in the case of small scale industries whereas in the case of cottage industries, majority of them faced with the problem of having very low or no status at all in the society.

TABLE 3.4 : Constraints faced by Rural Industries

(a) Self-sphere System
- Lack of leisure time
- Excessive workload
- Stress due to excessive workload.

(b) Socio-Psycho-System
- Social Status
- Recognition

(c) Resource System
- Lack of finance
- Lack of marketing
- Price variation
- Non-availability of raw materials
- Frequent shortage of raw materials
- Non-availability of modern technology
- Limited/non-availability of working capital

(d) Support System
- Inadequate promotional activities
- Inadequate financial assistance.

Resource System Constraints

Arrangements of finance (0.75 mean score), lack of marketing (0.78 mean score), price variation (0.72 mean score), sudden shortage of raw material (0.49 mean score), non availability of working capital, (0.64 mean score) are the main constraints.

Support System Constraints

Target oriented approach and inadequate promotional activities in Small Industry sector and inadequate financial assistance by Government and financial institutions in cottage industries were the main constraints.

The constraints faced by the Rural industries are represented in Table 3.4.

Discussion

Among the above mentioned four constraints, majority of the rural industries had expressed their major constraints as Resource system constraint which has been discussed in detail below :

Working Capital Requirements

The working capital requirements of the Rural Industries are not being met adequately by the financial institutes due to lack of knowledge about their requirements on the part of the proprietors/ partners.

Government Strictures

The Rural industries are facing too many visits and inspections by the Government officials regarding sales tax formalities and other such regulations and overemphasis by Government for implementing specifications for buildings, leading to high investments.

Non-availability of Labour

Even though labour is available, availability of skilled labours had been a problem which leads to wastage of material and time by educating them.

From the marketing aspect, the main problems identified are discussed below :

(a) *Packaging :* Since packaging of the producers are done on trial and error basis, the products are not appealing. Hence, competing with other established companies poses a problem in product appeal.
(b) *Pricing :* Due to frequent fluctuations in the raw material prices the product cannot be altered so frequently.
(c) *Selling :* Due to severe competition, rural industries are forced to sell their products at less remunerative prices thereby incurring losses.
(d) *Promotion :* In a stiff competitive market cost of advertisements and the call for literacy level in rural areas are so high that the rural industries are not able to afford to pay the price for the same.

(e) *Transport :* Although most of the rural areas are well connected by road, transportation of goods either in raw material form or in finished goods form becomes the problem and transporting in bulk involves storage and blockage of working capital.

(f) *Market Information :* The Rural Industries do not seem to have any adequate MIS and they seem to collect information on their own only, which do not allow them to have any new product decisions.

Conclusions and Recommendations

There always problem exist in rural industries and some face the problems as if they are challenges with the confidence that the problems are the road to advancement and growth. Therefore, the rural industrialists should be encouraged and made to feel and accept that they are a part of the largest society.

The problems of the rural industries are multi-dimensional. These problems can be solved by the co-ordinates efforts of the industries, promotional agencies and the Government Machineries.

The recommendations emerged out of this study may be considered by the concerned and implemented authorities for improving the performance of the Rural industries:

(1) Special concessions for the existing and the prospective industries for setting up units and simplifying and streamlining the procedure for availing of financial assistance and other special schemes, incentives etc.,

(2) Providing working capital at a low rate of interest for the deserving units after duly evaluating the viability of the unit,

(3) Providing a network of services like simple procedures for obtaining licence, other infrastructure facilities etc.

(4) Providing less specification for building thereby making less investments, and

(5) Providing a network for making produce from the rural industries as in the case of farm products — *uzhavar santhai.*

References

Business India, 1997.

Michael, V. P., *Research Methodology in Management,* Himalaya Publishing House, 1997.

Ramasamy and Namakumari, *Marketing Management and Concepts,* Macmillan Publishers.

Sinha , Jadunath, *Elementary Psychology,* New Central Book Agency, 1992.

4

PROBLEMS FACED BY SMALL SCALE PATTU SAREEES INDUSTRIES IN (MANAMPUSAVADI) PERIATHERU IN THANJAVUR TOWN

— *Madalai Mary* and *L. Kokila Devi*

Introduction

Cottage and small scale industries play a significant role in the development of the Economy, it contributes significantly to the national income and provides employment opportunities to a large number of people in rural economy. The available raw materials of the local area is used for production of goods and services. Moreover locally available tools and equipments are used in the production process. Capital shortage is the most important problem faced by Indian Economy in introducing latest technology in production. Too many problems are found in the establishment of large scale and medium scale industries by the country. 1948 and 1956 industrial policies had also given impetus for the establishment and growth of cottage and small scale industries in our economy. In modern times cottage and small scale industries are facing severe competition from large scale industries due to increased quantum of production.

The basis of distinction between the large scale, medium scale, small scale and cottage industries is generally the size, capital resource and labour force of the industrial unit. The difference between the small scale and cottage industries are basically two : (i) While small scale industries are mainly located in urban centres as separate establishment, the cottage industries are generally associated with agriculture and provide subsidiary employment in rural areas, and (ii) While small scale industries provide goods with partially or wholly mechanised equipment employing outside labour, the cottage industries involve operation mostly by hand which are carried on primarily with the help of the members of the family. The basis for cottage industries is thus one which is carried on wholly or primarily with the help of part-time occupation. A small scale industry on the other hand is one which is operated mainly with hired labour usually (Development and Regulation Act).

In order to understand the production and allied problems of small scale Pattu industries functioning in Periatheru (Manampusavadi) in Thanjavur town a case study is conducted. This area is very famous for its Pattu Sarees. In its production process and its course of its activities it faced a number of problems. According to 1991 census, Thanjavur district consisted of 20,28,960 population. Among them males were 10,28,000 and females were 10,00,960. 5,66,783 population were living in Thanjavur town. In the selected area of Periatheru the population were 1,20,000. Among them males were 62,560 and the remaining were female population.[1]

The people who are interested in Pattu Saree weaving is Saurashtra Community whose main occupation is Pattu Saree weaving. There are about 200 small units engaged in Pattu Saree weaving. Among them 40 small Pattu Saree weaving units are selected by simple random sampling. Nearly 80,000 people are engaged in these activities. Even educated males and females are engaged in this occupation. There are 9 streets in Periatheru area. In all the 9 streets Pattu Saree units are concentrated. At cottage level also certain units are functioning, but that are not taken into consideration in this study. Only small Pattu units that are engaging themselves in weaving Pattu Sarees alone taken into consideration.

From Table 4.1 it is understood that in eighth and ninth streets, more people are employed in Pattu Saree units. More units are also found to become small units and are employing less number of people and certain machinery mainly. Second and Sixth streets have 3 units each so people employed are also only 10 per cent. Selected number of units are 40 and number of people employed were 1600. So average people employed per unit are 40 in number. These units are having powerlooms and allied equipments. So they are able to produce more.

Table 4.1 : Selected Samples of Pattu Saree Units in Periatheru Street (Manampusavadi) in 1999

No. of Streets	No. of People Employed	No. of Units	Percentage of People employed
First Street	175	4	10.9
Second Street	160	3	10.0
Third Street	160	4	10.0
Fourth Street	200	6	12.5
Fifth Street	175	5	10.9
Sixth Street	160	3	10.0
Seventh Street	175	5	10.9
Eighth Street	200	5	12.5
Ninth Street	195	5	12.3
Total	1600	40	100.0

Investment

The amount of capital investment is averaged by 15 to 60 lakhs. Building, machinery and tools are brought in this categories. The circulating capital of the selected units are varying depending upon their sales and availability of raw materials ranging between 1 lakh to 2 lakhs. The machineries and tools are not imported.

Table 4.2 : Investment pattern of the sample units in the year 1999

Fixed Capital in Rs.	Working (in Rs. annual)	No. of Units	Percentage of Unit
15 lakhs to 30 lakhs	50000 - 1 lakh	10	25.00
30 lakhs to 45 lakhs	1 lakh -1.5 lakhs	15	37.50
45 lakhs to 60 lakhs	1.5 lakhs- 2 lakhs	15	37.50
Total		40	100.00

Among the 40 small scale units 15 units are having fixed capital of Rs. 45 lakhs to 60 lakhs and its working capital also varying Rs. 1.5 lakhs to 2 lakhs. That shows the increasing productivity of the small scale unit in the selected area. Another 15 units have a fixed capital of Rs. 30 lakhs to 45 lakhs and working capital is ranging between Rs. 1 lakh to 1.5 lakhs. These units are somewhat less in size than the previous units. They are trying to maximise their profit by producing more and satisfying the demand of the people. The last category is also able to meet the demands of the people. Even though capital investment capacity is varying, so all the selected 40 units are successful units and earning profit in 1999.

Production

There are different varieties of Pattu Sarees, namely LIC ordinary sarees demanded by most of the people in the historical town of Thanjavur. So the selected units are interested in weaving that type of sarees because each saree is capable of yielding Rs. 1000 as profit to the owners of units and self-designed sarees are also produced and sold and they are demanded by working women. So it is also yielding a profit of Rs. 4500 per saree. These sarees are very beautiful to look at. One-sided Jarigai Saree are demanded by middle and rich section of the people and they are capable of yielding Rs. 5000 as profit. Because these sarees are having durability, again the Jarigai could be sold for higher price after

Table 4.3 : Production of different varieties of Pattu Sarees by the sample units in 1999

Types of Sarees	Cost of Production in Rs.	Sales Price in Rs.	Profit Margin in Rs.
LIC Saree Ordinary Pattu Saree	1500 - 2500	2500 - 3500	1000
Self-deisgned Saree	3000 - 5000	7500 - 10500	4500
One-sided Jarigai Saree	5000 - 7000	10000 - 12000	5000
Double-sided Jarigai Grand Saree	15000 - 30000	21500 - 36500	6500

making use of it. The double-sided Jarigai sarees are demanded during the wedding seasons. They are ordered by the wedding parties. So, richer section of the people around the area, and their customers in Madras and other places are willing to buy these sarees. This type of sarees are very beautiful and it also has resale value. Thus the selected small scale units are producing various types of sarees and benefiting much.

Table 4.4 : Production details of Pattu Sarees by the selected units in 1999

No. of Units	No. of LIC Ordinary Pattu Saree	No. of Self-designed	No. of one-sided Jarigai Saree	No of Double-sided Jarigai Saree
12	100	70	100	NIL
8	158	85	120	8
6	206	90	155	10
14	256	105	200	19
Total	720	350	575	37

In the year 1999, the selected small scale units produced various types of sarees. 14 small scale units produced large number of all the four types of sarees, 12 units produced less number of all the three types of sarees. Remaining 6 units are producing moderately all types of sarees. Thus all the selected units carried on production in a systematic matter. The people who are working and handling machines are experts. So production is undertaken by all the units successfully well.

Among the 40 units, 12 units are recently started, viz. 5 years old and other 28 units have more than 10 years' experience in Pattu saree weaving. That is why nil production of double-sided sarees are not produced by the 12 units.

Profit / Loss

While analysing the working of the small scale units it is necessary to know about profit and loss condition of the selected units.

Table 4.5 : Profit and Loss details of the sample units in the year 1999

Annual Profit in amount Rs.	No. of units	Annual Loss in amount of Rs.	No. of units	Percentage of unit
50000 - 1 lakhs	6	0 - 20000	Nil	15
1 lakh - 1.5 lakhs	16	20000 - 40000	Nil	40
1.5 lakhs - 2 lakhs	8	40000 - 60000	Nil	20
2 lakhs - 2.5 lakhs	10	60000 - 80000	Nil	25
Total	40		Nil	100

From the above table it is understood that all the units are earning profits. No unit is incurring loss. 16 units earning an annual profit of Rs. 1 lakh to 1.5 lakhs and 10 units earning Rs. 2 lakhs to 2.5 lakhs profit. Thus Pattu Saree weaving is a productive work that is why in Periatheru among the 1,20,000 population 80,000 people are involved in Pattu Saree weaving activity. So 66.6 per cent of the people in this area engaged themselves in Pattu Saree weaving activity.

Problems

There are also certain problems faced by the people in Pattu Saree weaving. Like other industrial activities, Pattu Saree production also has its short- comings :

1. During rainy season it is very difficult to dye and dry the Pattu thread and Saree. So the quality of the saree is not good because of inadequate sunrays. Powercut is also another problem that is to be mentioned here. Because of these problems the quality of the sarees are becoming worse and they are fetching very low price, even though loss is compensated in other sarees weaved in non-rainy season.

Table 4.6 : Loss of the sample units due to rainy season is shown in the year 1998-99

Loss due to Quality Deterioration in Rs. (Annual)	No. of Units	Percentage of Units
10000 - 20000	18	45
20000 - 30000	16	40
30000 - 40000	6	15
Total	40	100

Usually Pattu Saree small scale units are reducing their production during rainy season. If at all they are getting more order for their sarees they are trying their level best in weaving it. But it is unavoidable they lose due to low quality of the sarees. 18 units incur an annual loss of Rs. 10000 to 20000 and 6 units to the extent of Rs. 30000 to 40000. Eventhough they are very careful but the loss is unavoidable.

2. Certain times employed labourers are taking leave and they delayed in weaving the sarees at correct time. This is also another problem faced by small scale Pattu unit owners.

3. The raw materials, Pattu thread is not available in certain period. This is also affecting the production of Pattu sarees. The availability of Pattu Jarigai, quality dye are also important for the beautiful look and combination of Pattu saree. The non-availability of the quality raw material is also another problem faced by Pattu saree units.
4. In selling also the producer of Pattu saree facing several problems. It is procured by the Pattu saree society on a large scale but the price is low considerably. If they sell it to private individuals, they can get high prices. In certain cases they are travelling far away from their production place to sell their sarees profitably but they have to face travelling charges, halting charges etc.
5. They face stiff competition from large scale industries which are producing Pattu sarees at cheap rates. Eventhough they have their own customers, they cannot sell more as large scale units are doing. Large scale units are involving themselves in advertising and sales promotion campaign. But it is beyond the reach of the small scale units as it involves large amount of money.
6. Finance is the crux of development of any activity. So these small scale units are not able to get finance from the banks in times of need. This is also another impediment in the process of production of Pattu sarees by small scale Pattu units in Periatheru (Manampusavadi) in Thanjavur town.

Conclusion

Pattu sarees are very famous in Manampusavadi, Thanjavur town because they are artistic and have beautiful designs. So most of the units are found in the area. Those people engaged in these activities are called as Saurashtra community. Small scale Pattu units are involving themselves in production very successfully, in spite of all the difficulties faced by them. So this study reveals well about the problem faced by small scale units in production and its allied activities.

5

PROBLEMS OF RURAL INDUSTRIES

— *V. M. Selvaraj*

Introduction

The progress of a country involves not merely economic but also social and institutional changes. In many underdeveloped countries, it calls for a new set of values and new concepts of society and government. India is a country of villages and so the development of the country mainly depends upon the all-round progress of the rural areas. Mahatma Gandhi, the Father of the Nation, wrote long back and said, " I have believed that India is to be found not in its few cities but in its 7,00,000 villages ..... I would say that if the villages perish, India will perish too." Rural development is advocated today as a basic strategy for all-round development of countries like India. In this context, the importance of rural industries is fully realised. Without proper development of rural industries, there cannot be any economic growth or social upliftment. The rural industries face a large number of problems, in this chapter, only a few problems are discussed.

Need for Rural Industrialisation

Rural industries play a vital role in the economy of our country.

After the completion of the Ninth Five Year Plan, today 23.7 per cent of the people still live below the poverty line. Much of this poverty arises due to lack of sufficient employment opportunities. Such poverty and unemployment problem can be tackled through rural industrialisation. The nature of unemployment problem in the rural areas clearly indicates that the problem can be successfully tackled through the rural industries. This is the only practical wayout.

Classification of Rural Industries

- Rural Industries
  - Cottage Industries
    - Handlooms
    - Handicraft
    - Sericulture
    - Khadi and village industries
      - Tiny Industries
      - Rural Artisans
      - Ancillary Industries
  - Small Scale Industries
  - Agro based Industries

For the purpose of this study, the Researcher has analysed various problems of Agro-based industries in Tirunelveli District.

Tirunelveli District At A Glance

This district is situated in southern part of Tamil Nadu, with a total area of 6816 sq. km. It lies between 8° 05′ and 9° 3′ of northern latitude and 77°'05′ and 78° 05′ of eastern latitude.

It is an agricultural region with 24.5 per cent of its geographical area under cultivation (2,17,718 hectares). Tamarabarani a perennial river is its major source for irrigation. Some streams which are seasonal, tanks and tube-wells also are other sources for irrigation. The most important crops grown in the district are Paddy, Cholam, Maize, Ragi, Cotton, Chillies, Pulse, Oil seeds, Sugarcane,

Banana, Cardamom, Arecanut and Tapioca. Paddy is the most important crop cultivated in 50 per cent of the cultivated area, 16 per cent Pulses and 10 per cent Cotton.

The district has dry and hot climate throughout the year. Normal rain fall is 940.7 mm. It receives rain from all the four seasons. It has red and black soil types.

About 1,25,508 hectares of land is under forest area. About 600 species of timber trees are grown in the district. Some of the wood varieties grown in the district are teak wood, wild jack, manjakadambu, venteak, vengai, pillaimaruthu, karimaruthu and bamboo. A good number of Palm trees are grown in the district. Wood-based industries are located in and around Shenkottai and Tenkasi taluks.

This district has a livestock population of

		Number
Cattle	=	4,28,354
Baffaloes	=	4,28,304
Goats and sheep	=	6,01,912
Fowls	=	6,53,172
Other animals	=	66,932

About 70,000 litres of milk is collected in the district from Palayamkottai and Sankarankoil. There are 257 dairy co-operative societies collecting milk for these two centres.

The department of Sericulture, Government of Tamil Nadu has plans to expand sericulture. They train farmers in mulberry cultivation, construction of rearing shed, silk realing and twining works. About 100 acres of area is under mulberry cultivation. Sericulture is mainly concentrated in Tenkasi, Kadayam, Kadayanallur, Ambasamudram and Shenkottai.

Ovari, Idinthakarai, Kutam are the fishing centres of Tirunelveli district.

Inland fish catch	-	2,947.56 MT
Marine fish catch	-	5,713.00 MT

Mainmuthar Dam has fish breeding centre, from here fingerlines are supplied to various fish farmers.

Banana, mango, citrus and guava are cultivated in this district. About 5 per cent of the total area cultivated comes under banana. Grapes and jack fruits are raised in limited areas. Potato, chillies, onions, carrot, ladies finger, beans, brinjal, grams and tapioca are some of the vegetables grown in this district. Vegetables are cultivated in 5 per cent of the cultivable area.

Limestone, graphite, garnet, red clay are some of the minerals available in this district. 35 million tonnes from land and 22 million tonnes of marine-based limestone is available. It is reported that 10,000 tonnes of graphite and 56,000 tonnes of garnet sand is also available.

This district has all the infrastructure and resources for the development of small scale industries. Major port (water transport) and airport at Tuticorin of Tuticorin district are added advantages for accelerating the industrial progress. As there are 22 large and medium scale industries there is a good scope for ancillary industries to meet the requirement of these industries by manufacturing components and spare parts.

The food processing industry tops the list of 55 units in the district and growth of this industry can be increased by increasing land available in the district. In view of availability of resources, the chemical, textile and forest-based industries have a good scope in this district.

Agriculture

India is primarily an agricultural country and the agricultural sector contributes nearly half of the national income. Seventy-five per cent of the total labour force is connected with agriculture. A large number of industries depend on agriculture and agricultural produce for their raw materials. These industries earn valuable foreign exchange. It is thus evident that the development of the Indian economy in a very large measure depends on the sound development of agriculture. But unfortunately agriculture in India is one, among the backward sectors. Farmers are illiterate, and the most primitive methods are used in agriculture. For their financial needs, the rural people depend on the village money-lenders who not only charge exorbitant rates of interest, but sometimes exploit their ignorance. Thus unknowingly they put themselves into a state of perpetual bondage. The Government of India allocates funds through co-operative societies to the rural sector in the Five Year Plans.

Agro-based Industries

Agro-based industries are those industries which obtain their major inputs from or which primarily meet the requirements of agricultural sector. The development of agro-based industries certainly will reduce the exodus of rural labour to urban centres and also improve the standard of living of rural communities.

Agro-based industries consist of two types of industries :

1. Agricultural processing and allied industries.
2. Industries producing inputs required for agriculture, animal husbandry and fishery etc.

But in practice, Agriculture processing and allied industries are considered to be Agro-based industries.

I. Agro-Food Based Industries

1. Aerated water/Synthetic syrups
2. Fruit juice - Mango and Lime
3. Guava cheese/jelly/toffee
4. Fruit Jams
5. Curry masala powder
6. Olcoresins from chillies
7. Groundnut oil
8. Coconut oil
9. Desiccated Coconut
10. Coconut shell powder
11. Potato wafers/chips

12. Banana powder
13. Palmyrah based products
14. Coir and coir based products.
15. Peanut candy
16. Ragi malt
17. Bakery
18. Confectionery

II. Marine-based Industries

1. Freezing of Prawn/Shrimps/Lobster
2. Canned fish
3. Bromine
4. Light basic magnesium carbonate
5. Plaster of Paris
6. Fishing float
7. Cattle lick salt
8. Dairy salt
9. Iodised salt

III. Mineral-based Industries

1. Bricks
2. Roofing tiles
3. Hydrated lime
4. Precipitated calcium carbonate
5. Lime colours

IV. Livestock-based Industries

1. Fished leather
2. Leather tanning
3. Leather footwear
4. Leather goods
5. Bone meal
6. Meat processing and packing

V. Forest-based Industries

1. Splints and veneer
2. Mechanised boats
3. Wooden furniture
4. Cane furniture
5. Wooden toys, brush, handle etc.,

VI. Demand-based Industries

1. Calcium carbide
2. Dyes and dye intermediaries
3. Drugs and Pharmaceuticals
4. Camphor tablets
5. Bicycle parts and components
6. Tyre retreading
7. Improved agricultural implements
8. Repairing and servicing automobiles
9. Electric motors repairing and rewinding
10. PVC pipes upto 110 mm dia
11. Cardboard from waste paper
12. Wooden trays, racks, frames etc., for safety match industry
13. Spare parts for motor pumps
14. Tooth powder
15. Paints
16. Potassium bicarbonate
17. Tubelight fittings
18. Hand-made paper
19. Mineral grinding
20. Blue metal jelly

Among these industries, Rice making, Blue metal jelly making, gem powder producing are the most popular industries in Tirunelveli, Kattabomman District.

Problems of Agro-based Industries

There are a number of problems faced by the Agro-based industries. The Researcher has conducted a survey to know the problems that are faced by Agro-based industries. The Researcher has selected 100 respondents in the district. On the basis of information and answers given by them the Researcher has summarised the important problems only.

Poor Availability of Raw Material

Many of the agro-based industries find it difficult to obtain the right type of raw materials at the right time and at moderate prices. Agricultural produce are seasonal products. Agro-based industries suffer from this problem due to their poor financial position. They cannot stock adequate raw materials when they are available. Agro-based industries obtain their inputs from agricultural sector. The output of agricultural sector depends upon the soil, climatic conditions, rainfall, use of fertilizers, pesticides etc.. Therefore, agricultural output cannot be increased according to the demands of agro-based industries. Therefore, agro-based industries face the problem of inadequate raw materials. The quantity of raw materials available from agricultural sector may not be adequate sometimes, the agro based industries cannot or may not get the supply in time. The quality of agricultural commodities cannot be controlled by the agriculturists. Sometimes, inferior quality of agricultural commodities are cultivated. The inferior quality of agricultural crops would affect the quality of agro- based industries. In case of Rice making mill, the success of the industries depends upon the cultivation of paddy. Cultivation of paddy depends upon sufficient rainfall, use of fertilizer, pesticides, soil of the land etc. Among these factors, rainfall is the main and important factor which affects the cultivation of paddy. Here, the rainfall is not enough to produce the paddy during the seasons. Due to this factor, these industries operate at 40 per cent capacity. A few industries are sick industries. These sick industries refuse to give sufficient information for their sickness and to revive the business.

Blue Metal Jelly making industries depend upon the extraction of Blue Metal from the land. But these are natural resources. Blue metal is depleting year by year, due to this, the number of these industries are decreasing year by year. But there is no heavy demand for Blue Metal Jelly. To overcome this problem, Blue Metal may be purchased from other districts which have sufficient Blue Metal.

Gem powder producing industries are also seasonal industries and these industries depend upon the natural resources. The availability of the raw material for these industries is also insufficient. Almost 70 to 80 per cent of rural industries face many problems. Among the problems, poor availability of raw materials is the main problem. It is to be solved by the authority concerned.

The Problem of Capital

Capital is one among the four factors of production. No industry can function without capital. Capital is necessary to carry on productive activities. Capital is also necessary for development and expansion. Therefore, capital is the life blood for every business. Owners of Agro- based industries do not have sufficient capital. They cannot obtain adequate financial assistance from the financial institutions. Because they do not have right type of security which is demanded by the financial institutions as collateral security. So for their financial requirements, they often go to many lenders who charge exorbitant rates of interest. Money lenders constitute the main source of rural credit. In India the share of Non- Institutional credit is 42.6 per cent. It is apt to refer here to a caustic French proverb which says that "Credit supports the farmers as the hangman's rope supports the hanged". They sell out their finished products at low price in order to obtain sufficient funds so that they may pay the interest at instalments for the money lenders. The owners of agro-based industries live a hand to mouth existence. Agro-based industries come under the category of priority sector lendings. Financial assistance is provided to agro-based industries. But, the assistance is not given at the right time and at right quantity.

Poor Transport Facilities

Agro-based industries face the problem of poor transport facilities. Development of transport facilities is inadequate. In some rural areas, there is no proper roads to transport the output of agro-based industries. The demand for the products is very low in rural areas. The cost of transport also results in an increase in prices. Hence, the products are sold in the local areas at low price.

Irregular availability of power

Agro-based industries face the problem of irregular supply of power. In many rural villages, power is not at all available. So, they have to use manpower to produce the commodities. Manpower is very costly. Therefore, the cost of production is high. At the same time, they are unable to sell their products at a profit.

From the survey, the Researcher has obtained the following results :

Sl. No.	Problems	No. of Respondents	Percentage to total
1.	Poor availability of raw materials	50	50
2.	Problem of capital	16	16
3.	Poor transport facilities	18	18
4.	Irregular availability of power	6	6
5.	Others	10	10

Source : Computed from primary data.

Suggestions

Following suggestions are given to eliminate the problems of agro-based industries :

1. Steps may be taken to improve the quality and quantity of agricultural products. If they are improved, then the agro-based industries may get sufficient quantity and quality of raw materials for their operation.
2. The road facilities are to be improved to all rural areas.
3. Some of the entrepreneurs are unaware of the provision of financial help for agro-based industries. Sufficient steps must be taken to improve the financial help to agro-based industries.
4. Infrastructural facilities are to be improved in rural areas to some extent.

Conclusion

Agro based industries face many problems. It is essential to remove the problems of agro-based industries. Today the Government has put maximum efforts to the growth of rural industries. If the above problems are solved, then employment opportunities will be increased by way of self-employment to both literate and illiterate persons.

References

Alak Ghosh, *Indian Economy — Its Nature and Problems,* The World Press Private Limited, Calcutta, 1971, pp. 211.

Bepin Behari, *Current Economic Problems,* p. 259.

Gandhiji, quoted in Radha Raman Singh and Rabindra Narayan Singh, *IRDP and Revitalisation of Rural Scene in India,* Khadi Gramodyog January, 1985, pp. 172.

6

PROBLEMS OF RURAL INDUSTRIES : A Case Study in Chidambaram Taluk

— *C. Madhavi, C. Samudhara Rajakumar* and *M. Syed Zafar*

Introduction

Economic development of any country demands industrialization. Though it has got recognition in our country, it is high time to think about balanced regional development, an important component of industrialisation. Rural development forms a key component in a nation's progress towards economic freedom and equality. But, mobilization of rural people towards cities and ineffective utilisation of rural resources stand as hurdles in the rural development. Hence, it is very important to develop and encourage rural industries. Further, it needs to be equipped to face the new challenges due to economic reforms and changing technology.

In spite of glaring frontal growth during half century period, truly speaking rural India has remained in the scenario of miseries only. In the countryside, agriculture cannot provide work for all throughout the year. Both unemployment and underemployment indirectly acts as a major cause for communal clashes and other criminal activities.

The land space of India is 2.4 per cent of the world, wherein 4.4 per cent of the population live. In India, presently 629 million are from rural areas constituting 74.3 per cent. High population is one of the reasons for poor economic status. 7.5 crores are unemployed in rural areas. Hence, rapid development of non-farm sector is the only answer for creation of job opportunities. It is right time to launch massive programme for revamping of the rural industrialization on activities, viz., cottage, village, tiny and micro units through adoption of business strategies so that the sector can provide gainful employment in rural areas.

High illiteracy rate in rural areas is another setback of rural India. In this social situation, what India needs today more than anything else is economic self-sufficiency. This is possible only by uplifting rural India through rural industrialisation. But, globalisation seriously affects the traditional economic strategies of self-reliance and economic sovereignty. It will be hard to encounter the challenges of globalisation. If the development of the nation is contingent upon uplifting the rural poor and labour class, then its marginalisation in the process of globalisation poses a challenge to India's economic management.

Village-oriented viable projects are needed to give our youth fitting jobs and make them independent partners of an economically sound and secured society. It is a known fact that attainment of economic independence must begin from the grassroot level, the village. No one foresaw this better than Gandhiji. His concept of *Gram Swaraj* as envisioned through the *Charkha,* forms a fundamental element. Gandhi's constructive programme is the result of the synthesis between the moral and material advancement of human society. Presently, village and small industries sector contributes 35 per cent of the gross value of the output in the manufacturing sector and 40 per cent of the total exports in the country with an employment level of 12 million.

Five Year Plans and Rural Industries

Government recognises the importance of uplifting rural India and also has taken much effort to develop rural areas. During the Third Five Year Plan, Government of India proposed Rural

Industrialisation Programme (RIP) for setting up industries in rural areas. Fourth and Fifth Five Year Plans further added introduction of incentive schemes, subsidy etc. Sixth Plan stressed on rural development particularly on rural industries through an integrated rural development approach wherein all sectors of rural economy and all special purpose State development schemes were taken up for development.

Seventh Plan stressed the importance to check the exodus of rural artisans to urban concentration. Strengthening of infrastructure facilities, application of modern management techniques, development and dissemination of appropriate technology, skill quality and productivity improvement were some of the measures led to considerable success in khadi industries. For the Eighth Plan (1992-97) outlay on rural development has been enhanced to 300,000 million from Rs. 49,000 million for the Seventh Plan. Actual expense was 320,000 million. The total outlay for different industries of small scale was 2784.5 crores. Based on this plan scope for new small scale industries were enlightened. Plan outlay of Eighth Five Year Plan is shown in Table 6.1.

Table 6.1 : Plan Outlay of Eighth Five Year Plan

Sl. No.	Industry	Rs. in crores
1.	Small Scale Industry	692
2.	Khadi and Village Industry	900
3.	Coir Looms	30
4.	Hand Looms	621
5.	Power Looms	18
6.	Sericulture	270
7.	Handicrafts	223
8.	Wool Development	20
9.	NIFT (Textile)	5
10.	Others	5.5

Source : Annual Plan Report, Planning Commission.

Village Industry refers to any industry located in a rural area, village or town with a population upto 20,000 with less capital investment on plant and machinery. 76 such industries are identified which are grouped in seven categories such as mineral based industry, forest based industry, agro based, polymer and chemical based, engineering and non-conventional energy, textile industry and service scheduled industry. But, rural industries though established in rural areas are essentially industrial enterprises. These enterprises are dependent on rural products, though they can as well be sited in urban areas. Rural enterprises generally comprise dairies and sugar factories.

The Khadi and Village Industries Commission (KVIC) was established by an Act of Parliament, is mainly a service organisation engaged in the promotion and development of Khadi and Village industries in rural areas, with the objective of (a) Skill improvement, (b) employment in rural areas, (c) transfer of technology, (d) promoting self-reliance and (e) rural industrialisation.

The Small Industries Development Organisation (SIDO) also started functioning with the following objectives :

(a) Village industries must be strengthened to generate more job opportunities.
(b) Training for technology and quality.
(c) Technology development and upgradation.
(d) Credit availability.
(e) Institutional mechanisms will have to be evolved for augmentry credit flow to informal and rural non-farming sector.

Problems of Rural Industries

The future of India lies on the level of teeming rural million. She can develop only from a progressive growing and dynamic rural society. Small Scale and Cottage industries play an important role under the peculiar Indian conditions. They contribute about half of the gross value of output originating in the manufacturing sector. They help in employment generation, reducing economic inequalities, mobilizing latest resources of capital and enterprises, regional dispersal of industries and maintaining harmonious industrial relations and contribute to exports.

The present small scale industry includes modern small scale industries, handloom, handicrafts, coir, natural skill, looms and village industries.

Rural Industrialists face problems such as inadequate finance, outdated technology, inefficient management, competition from large scale industries, power shortage, etc.

Mainly there is fierce competition in the market from the products of modern factories. Our Nobel Laureate Amartya Sen had also pointed out in one of his works, how khadi is losing in the battle without the choice of technology. The cost of products manufactured through mechanised process will be comparatively less than the cost of products made manually.

It is pathetic to observe that attitude of rural people is to send children to work when there is scope to work in rural industries. It ultimately acts as a hurdle in the development of society as a whole. Privatisation and globalisation acts as a serious threat on rural industry survival. Whenever, modern technology has been adopted, the first casuality has always been the handicrafts and skill based activities.

This situation now demands urgent remedial measures for the existing anomalies as also steps to revitalise and expand the small-scale village and cottage industries.

Scope for Rural Industries

The main stay of the perspective is the locational approach which results in dispersal or relocation of industries in rural areas. The approach does not take into account the situational factors present in the area and consequences of industrialisation is rural area.

The scope is wide when the importance is given to resource based industries supported by appropriate product structure, scale of operation and technology. Revival of hand spinning and weaving, would make the largest contribution to the economic and moral regeneration of India. Similarly, sericulture can also contribute much.

Entries of MNCs in India is mainly due to less labour cost. Further, Indians go abroad and take up some labour which they are hesitant to do in their own country. There is a scope to use this resource effectively in rural industries. Government can sponsor people to get trained in the area of their interest and to establish units relating to the products which are of high demand.

Scope is very bright for good quality of yarn handloom sector. The whole world is facts moving towards 100 per cent cotton clothes because of the harm caused by synthetic. This being the situation there is much scope for handlooms. Similarly, there is craze for handicrafts. A proper education and training accompanied by a strong marketing strategy would earn for Indian workers enormous funds.

We have Amul — a success story in the rural areas of Gujarat. Keeping this as a model, other such possible fields should be identified and developed so as to stay afloat in the new order. Rural units can also think of value added products based on the resource availability in that location.

Year 2000, being the platinum jubilee of the birth of khadi, there is lot of scope to take khadi to international trade, if properly handled. According to the handbook of Industry, 'Policy and Statistics', export of silk goods, handicrafts, gems, jewellery, sericulture, coir products handloom products, etc., keep on increasing census of handlooms of India by Ministry of Textiles. It shows that Tamil Nadu stands second in the number of handloom units in rural area. This can be extended to other areas also.

Following viable units can be thought of: Extracting edible Non-edible oil, Animal Husbandry, Pisciculture, Renewable energy harnessing, Bio-fertilizer conversion units, Building materials production, Rubber and leather goods, mineral based products, forest based units, coir, tobacco, ceramics, etc.

A Case Study in Chidambaram Taluk

Rural development can be attained by maximising production in agriculture and allied activities, development of rural industries which ultimately improve the standard of living. When there is enormous scope for developing rural industries it is rightly important to identify the existing problems of rural industries and also to take necessary measures to overcome the problems.

The main objectives of this study are :

* to identify the problems of rural industries, and
* to make an attempt to suggest measures to improve the present position.

Since our study is confined to a small place, enough care must be taken while generalising the results. The sample size is also very much small. It was also very difficult to get the confidence of the respondent to get unbiased response.

To study the above mentioned objectives, an empirical study was carried out. A sample of 25 entrepreneurs conveniently chosen is Chidambaram taluk. A structured schedule was used to collect the necessary data relating to the objectives. Percentage and ANOVA were used to analyse the data collected.

The Major Findings of the Study are summarised below

Thirty per cent of the entrepreneurs in rural area belongs to below-poverty line. Hardly any change occurs, the situation is worse and they find themselves in distress. Table 6.2 shows the problems encountered by the entrepreneurs of rural industries.

Financial Problems

All the respondents expressed that the problems relating to finance was felt very high. They also expressed that working capital (95%) was more complex than that of capital (88%).

Production Problems

Among the production oriented problems, 90 per cent of the respondents identified power-cut as the major problem. The next one was implementation of technology in rural areas which was supported by 81 per cent. Other problems related to production were availability of spare parts, quality maintenance and cost of production which were endorsed by 76.4, 36.8 and 44.40 per cent respectively.

Table 6.2 : Intensity of problems in rural industries

Factors	Mean value	Percentage
Financial		
a. Capital	4.40	88.0
b. Working capital	4.75	95.0
Production		
a. Technology implementation	4.05	81.0
b. Spare parts availability	3.82	76.4
c. Power-cut	4.50	90.0
d. Quality Maintenance	1.84	36.8
e. Cost of production	2.22	44.4
Personnel		
a. Labour cost	4.06	81.2
b. Labour problem	3.24	64.8
c. Availability of skilled personnel	3.48	49.6
Marketing		
a. Promotion	3.26	65.2
b. Product development	3.75	75.0
c. Advertising	2.04	40.8
Others		
a. Transport	2.02	40.4
b. Communication	1.56	31.2
c. Storage	3.25	65.0
d. Banking	1.40	28.0
e. Administrative problems	3.92	78.4
f. Information availability	1.94	38.8

Source : Computed from primary data.

Personnel Problems

Major problems pertaining to personnel area were identified as labour cost, labour problem and availability of skilled personnel. Labour cost was identified as the highly problematic issue. 81.2 per cent of the respondents felt that labour cost as very important problem in the area of personnel. The next factor was labour problems which was endorsed by 64.8 per cent of the respondents. Labour problems mean irregular work, disobedience, being tough etc. Apart from that, getting skilled personnel was identified as another issue which was supported by 49.6 per cent of the respondents.

Marketing problems

The problems identified in the area of marketing were promoting the products, product development and advertisement. Among these factors 75 per cent of the sample expressed product development is a very difficult task. Then promoting the products was found to be problematic as a very difficult task. Then promoting the products was found to be problematic which was endorsed by 65.2 per cent of the respondents. 40.8 per cent of the sample felt that advertising is not essential.

Apart from the problems relating to the functional areas of business, other problems were administrative problems, storage facility, information availability, area of operation, transport, communication and banking facilities. These factors were endorsed by 78.4 per cent, 65 per cent, 40.4 per cent, 38.8 per cent, 31.2 per cent and 28 per cent of the sample respectively.

Administrative problems might cover problems pertaining to decision making, planning, co-ordination, leading, motivation, etc. Information may be relating to legal factors, productivity improvement, skill development market changes, standardization, regulations etc.

40.4 per cent of the respondents expressed that transport was found to be expensive. It might be due to poor service and poor road conditions. Information about different markets at proper tie was felt as an important hurdle in the development of rural industries. This view was endorsed by 38.8 per cent of the respondents.

31.2 per cent of the respondents expressed that one of the major issues of rural industries was concerned with communication problem. Further, 28 per cent of the respondents identified even banking services was inadequate.

In the first phase, multi-dimensions of rural industries were discussed. In the second phase, further attempt was made to know whether the view on these factors differ significantly based on age, generation in business and education.

Age and Personnel factors

Because of the small sample size the respondents were grouped into two categories based on their age. Respondents between the age 22 and 35 were grouped into one category and the second category of respondents were between 36 and 52.8 and 17 respondents were found to be in the first and second category respectively. ANOVA was carried to test whether there was any significant difference between the two groups. The probability value was found to be 0.0429. It implies that the view of the respondents relating to personnel factors varied significantly. The intensity of problems felt regarding personnel factors listed for this study varied significantly at 5 per cent level. Since the mean value of the respondents in the first category was less that the mean value of the second group, it could be concluded that, the elderly people viewed personnel problems more complicated than that of the younger generation.

Generation in Business

Attempt was made to identify whether there was any significant difference between the first generation in the business and the respondents in the business with more than the generation. The factors which differed were marketing and finance.

19 respondents were new to the field whereas for the remaining 6, their family was already in the business. The probability value derived by applying ANOVA was 0.0439. Hence, a significant level of different was observed between the two at 5 per cent level. Mean value for the first generation was high and it could be derived that the new entries found it more problematic to market their products.

Similarly, views about 'finance' factors by these groups were also studied. The result of ANOVA implied that (Prob. Value 0.0413) the observed significant level intensity of the problem relating to finance. From the mean values of the two groups it could be concluded that the first generation entering into business, found it more problematic than those whose business was family business.

Education

Factors such as 'administration' and 'availability of information' were found to differ significantly based on the education level. Diploma holders, graduates and above were considered as one group and those who were with school education were formed another group. There found a significant level of difference between them relating to administrative problems and availability of information. The probability values are 0.298 and 0.353. Respondents with less education level found that administrative was more problematic comparatively. Educated people might be knowing how to get the things done. Further, they could easily be able to collect the relevant information relating to their business.

Suggestions

Based on the above findings the following suggestions are made for the upliftment of rural industries.

To minimize the financial problem, authorities can minimize the time taken for loan sanctioning and ensure the loan at the time of requirement.

Funding alone is not sufficient, to make it economically viable, it is important to make radical changes associated with regulating production, marketing project etc. Expert committee can be formed to discuss the plans and strategies of the rural entrepreneurs.

In order to encourage rural industries, government can suggest viable projects suitable to the area, in addition to funding the projects.

It is the responsibility of the government to provide uninterrupted supply of power.

Rural co-operative federation and non-government organisation can help by providing information relating to product and process so as to improve technology, availability of spare-parts, quality improvement and cost-reduction. It is necessary to ensure flexibility in operations for launching innovative products according to market requirement. Mini industrial estate for village may be implemented. Cluster approach in several pockets can help in technical guidance also. The point of reference for R & D efforts should be field related operational problems and this must be extended by government.

For improving productivity, imparting knowledge for the employees in rural industries is also suggested. Further artisans are to be trained to develop their skills and also equip themselves to design items according to the tastes and preferences of consumers in different markets such as rural and urban, national and international.

To motivate the first generation entrepreneurs and to encourage rural industrialisation, management institution and government must extend help in marketing the products. Markets are not friendly and it keeps changing. It is necessary to ensure flexibility on operation for launching innovative products according to market requirement to reduce the marketing risk. To minimize the marketing problem it is also suggested to initiate co-operative organisation in rural areas.

There is wide scope for hand made products and to explore the international market I.T. can be used. It is suggested that government should create a website, for such products at free of cost to get the benefits of direct sales and earn foreign exchange.

It is better to plan for integrated rural development programmes relating to market trends, lending agencies and improved technologies for successful business activity.

Government apart from suggesting gainful projects to rural entrepreneurs, it can further encourage them to enter into value added projects.

Services relating to market news, standardisation, trading, etc., can also be extended to rural industries. I.T can also help in reaching business information on day to day changes.

Conclusion

It is basically important to stress for sustainable rural industrialisation in policies and implementation to ensure job opportunities and gradual improvement in the quality of life in the rural areas. There is no second opinion that non-farm sector is the only answer for not only tackling the gigantic unemployment scenario but also for avoiding regional imbalance. So the call of the day is "Rapid Rural Industrialisation". Survival and development of rural industries is possible only by hard work.

Scope

There are a number of dimensions where further research can be studied. Comparison of problems of entrepreneurs can be made based on district level and State level. Comparing the exclusive problems of different industries might produce interesting results. In future, awareness level of entrepreneurs will increase and the problems will be micro in nature and that further increases the scope.

References

Bandyopadhyay, S., "Rural Industrialisation in Millennium", *Khadi Gramodyog,* Vol. 46, November 99.

Lahiry, S.C., "Rural Industrialisation - An overview", *Kurukshetra,* August 1997.

Pandit Rao, Y.A, "Issues Relating to Rural Industrialisation in India", *Khadi Gramodyog,* Vol. 46, July 2000.

Rao, G.U.K. and Krishna, P.V., "Cottage and Village Industries in Nalanda", *Khadi Gramodyog,* Vol. 26, February 1983.

Research Highlights published by National Institute of Rural Development, Govt. of India, 1997-98.

Rural Development Statistics, published by NIRD, 1998.

7

RETROSPECT AND PROSPECT OF FOOD PROCESSING INDUSTRY

— *P. M. Meera Mohiadeen*

Prelude

Food processing in India is a very old industry. It was only after the announcement of New Industrial Policy in 1991, that the food processing industry was identified as one of the high priority areas. It further gained momentum when the confederation of Indian Industries (CII) and noted management consultant firm Mckinsy drafted the Food and Agricultural Integrated Development Report (FAIDA) in 1997. The report estimated that the value added food market would reach a whopping Rs. 2,25,000 crore (mainly the instant food and atta) by the year 2005. Fruit and vegetables production was also identified as a major growth area.

As of now, India is the second largest producer of fruits and vegetables in the world after China and accounts for 9 per cent of the total world output. Similarly in the case of the wheat production, India is the second largest producer in the world and wheat production rose sharply from 65.9 million tonnes in 1997-98 to 72.0 million tonnes in 1998-99 (See Table 7.1). Foodgrain production in 1998-99 was 203 million tonnes. But during the year 1999-2000 the same level of the output is not possible due to erratic and inadequate rainfall in some States.

Based on the present consumption pattern the total requirements of foodgrains will be the present consumption pattern the total requirement of foodgrains will be around 220.5 million tonnes and 243.2 million tonnes for 2001-2002 and 2006-2007 respectively.

Table 7.1 : Wheat Production

Year	Gross Area (in Million Hectares)	Output (in Million Tonnes)
1994-1995	25.7	65.8
1995-1996	25.0	62.1
1996-1997	25.9	69.4
1997-1998	26.7	65.9
1998-1999	27.0	72.0

Source : Economic Survey 1998-1999.

For these two periods the demand for edible oils, milk, vegetables and fruits will be 7.9 and 9.5 million tonnes, 93.1 and 119.5 million tonnes and 93.6 and 110.7 million tonnes and 53.7 million tonnes 70.5 million tonnes respectively. Similarly, 30-40 per cent increases are required in case of the marine and livestock products from the present level of 5.4 and 3.6 million tonnes. However, in the case of fruits and vegetables, only 1.6 per cent of the products has been processed in India as against 83 per cent in Malaysia, 78 per cent in Philippines and 70 per cent in Brazil. Hence , there is a great potential for processing industry. Further, it reveals that it is one of the least exploited areas of business opportunities.

Importance of Food Processing Industry

The need for the development of food processing industry is not only argued on the basis of the above factors but also the following important factors :

(a) This industry directly employs more than 1.6 million people in the food processing industry and also has immense scope for employment generation in other industry. For instance, a study on Annual Survey on Industries shows that consumer goods such as foods have an employment elasticity of 0.9. This means that if output in these industries were to double, employment would increase by 90 per cent. (See Table 7.2).

Table 7.2 : Employment of food processing industry since liberalization

(March 1991-1997)

Sub-sector	Approvals (Joint Ventures, Foreign Collaborations, Industrial Licences and 100% Export-oriented units)		Industrial Memoranda	Entrepreneurs (IEMs)	Total Employment
	Number	Employment	Number	Employment	
Urban	80	15,000	563	59,000	74,000
Non-Urban	880	2,42,000	3,392	5,72,000	8,14,000
Total	960	2,57,000	3,395	6,31,000	8,88,000

Note : Employment in number of persons. These are cumulative figures since liberalization. (March 1991-97).

Source : Press Information Bureau, Government of India.

(b) This industry has responsible for the growth of number of other industries like transportation, pesticides and fertilizers, warehousing and refrigeration in direct and indirect form.

(c) It requires very low level of capital amount. The government give top priority to agricultural activities on par with the telecommunication and power sector.

(d) The excise duty has been completely removed from diary equipment and has been reduced from 10 per cent to 8 per cent on certain items like biscuits. Further the government removed some of the items like biscuits manufacturing, rice milling, dal milling and poultry feed that were previously reserved for the small scale sector.

(e) India's processed food export has been increasing in the recent past. It is evident from Table 7.3 that the processed food was increased from Rs. 932.4 crores during the year 1995-96 to

Rs.1302.5 crores during the year 1996-97. Further, there is a huge potential for processed food products' export. As the GATT Laws on agriculture come into effect in 2005, it will provide further scope to Indian processed food product exports. Because Agriculture in developed countries is highly subsidised. Indian processed foods, not used to subsidied, will have competitive price in the Post GATT scenario (See Table 7.3) .

Table 7.3 : India's Processed Food Exports

(Rs. in crores)

Items	1995-1996	1996-1997
Fruits and Juices	204.6	224.6
Vegetables	142.7	106.8
Spirits & Vegetables	44.7	200.0
Miscellaneous items	540.4	771.1
Total	932.4	1302.5

Source: Import-Export Business Magazine — Global August 1997.

In spite of the above advantageous factors, the investment in food processing industry has remained very low levels compared to other manufacturing industries. Hence, this chapter focuses the reasons for slow penetration and problems to be faced by the food processing industrial units.

The study is based on the secondary sources of information and the data collected from CII-Mckinsey FAIDA Report, CMIE/ Industry Report, Press Information Bureau, Government of India, *Economic Survey, Hindu Survey* on Agriculture and Industries. *The Economic Times and Financial Express Investment Weekly* etc.

Problems

1. *Complacency of Entrepreneurs :* Seventy-five per cent of the entrepreneurs belongs to unorganized small scale sectors. The Union Budget of 1997-98 activates further to start the food processing industry in small scale level. For instance, as per the Union Budget (1997-98), the units with a turnover of up to 30 lakh will attract no duty, while those in the range of 30-50 lakh will have to pay a fixed duty of 3 per cent and above 50

lakh will attract 5 per cent duty. This move has hindered the growth of the food processing industry. The entrants will prefer to enter the small scale sector to avoid excise duty, and this will in turn increase the size of the unorganized sector. The existing small scale players are also not has an interest to move to higher scale of operation to retain the excise duty benefit.

2. *Brand Building :* The new entrant as well as the existing entrepreneurs found in difficulties to cope with existing or well established companies' brands or multinationals' brands. For the brand building exercise they either should cut the price at the entry level itself or spend huge amount of expenditure for advertising and marketing. This is not possible for all the entrepreneurs.
3. *Excise Crunch :* The Central Government tax on the food and food processing equipments is still much higher than in most nations. Table 7.4 reveals that the total tax burden on processed foods stand at around at 16 per cent in India, whereas it is only 10 per cent in most of the Asian countries. Further, India imposes an excise duty in the range of 19 to 40 per cent on capital goods, while no other country in Asia charges excise on capital goods. In the case of the cold storage and processing equipment, import duties lie in the range of 20-50 per cent, it is nearly five times the Malaysian rentals. The cumulative tax burden on packaged milk and atta is 13 per cent and 8 per cent respectively. In other countries, such foods are considered as essential dietary items and often bear no taxation.

Table 7.4 : Taxation in Food Processing

(Figures in Percentage)

Name of the Country	Value Added		Capital Equipment	
	Excise	Sales	Excise	Sales
Malaysia	Nil	Nil	Nil	Nil
Thailand	Nil	7	Nil	5
Indonesia	Nil	12	Nil	5-15
Philippines	Nil	10	Nil	10-20
India	8-40	5-12	10-40	20-50

Source : ICII-Mickinsey FAIDA Report.

4. *Denial of Modvat Benefit* : The food processing industry is using various raw materials and other items for the manufacture of the goods. These items are already tax involved. Therefore, the food processing industry eligible to avail the Modvat benefits. But the government has not permitted it to avail the benefits.
5. *Too many authorities to control* : The food processing industry under the control of various authorities like Ministry of Food Processing, Ministry of Agriculture and Ministry of Industries etc., The Mckinsey report has identified more than 20 laws relating to the food sector in the country. This inevitably leads to numerous problems in terms of implementation of policy and control. For instance, Fruit Product Order (FPO) and other laws determine production specifications and quality control requirements. The too much restraint of the FPO certainly curtails the interest of the small scale entrepreneurs to start the food processing industry. Further, this restraint the food processing companies to change their products according to the market requirements.
6. *Reservation* : Traditionally, food processing has been limited to the small scale and cottage industries. Three-fourth processing output in India is controlled by these industries. The owners of these units neither has the interest to grow nor the resources to do business in large scale. These small scale entrepreneurs seldom adopt the latest technology, because the Government has protected the small entrepreneurs by way of reservation of several food sectors for small scale and cottage industries' production.
7. *Technology Up-gradation* : As the majority of the players belong to small scale industries and have limited amount of capital, they are not in a position to upgrade the technology. The technology upgradation will require huge amount of investment. As a result the quality of the product is substandard.
8. *Unfavourable Perception* : In general, the majority of the urban people have the ability to buy and use the processed food items. The rural population either not have enough knowledge how

to use the processed items or they are not having the habit of using the processed food items. One of the reason is that they have the food items at their doorsteps itself. Further, they like to take hot breakfast such as chappati, roti and iddely instead of cold and crispy one. The rural as well as urban people have the perception that "fresh is best".

Hence, they normally use the fresh food items, fresh fruits and vegetables. This type of unfavourable perception of the Indian masses will hamper the growth of the food processing industry. To change the perception favourably to the needs of the operators they will incur huge amount of expenditure for aggressive advertising and marketing.

9. *Large number of Intermediaries:* The Indian food industry is characterized by a large number of intermediaries in between the farmer to the end user (See Chart 7.1). This will increase

Chart 7.1 : Showing the intermediaries in the food chain

Farmer
↓
Consolidator
↓
Commission Agents
↓
Trader
↓
Commission Agent
↓
Wholesaler
↓
Retailer

the cost of food items. For example, the prices of vegetables triple between the farmer and the end user. Further, in the process of transportation of fruits and vegetables, the operators will incur additional expenditure due to the long chain and the food items may be deteriorated.

10. *Power-cut :* Another major problem faced by the food processing industry is the power-cut. This will not only create problems in storage of the food items but also in manufacturing of the goods.
11. *High Packing Cost :* Worldwide, the cost of packaging is much lower at 20 per cent whereas in India it is around 45-55 per cent of the cost of production. This is another major problem to the Indian food processing industry. This will increase the cost of production and reduces the profitability of entrepreneur.
12. *Shelf Life :* The shelf life of the packaged flour in India is typically 15-20 days whereas it is in U.S.A. six months to one year. It not only disturbs the distribution network of the company but also restricts from capturing distant new markets and the quality of the product is also deteriorated. As a result, the consumers are dissatisfied with the product.
13. *Inadequate Infrastructure Facilities :* There is an urgent need for established cold storage and warehousing facilities by the public sector in a large scale manner. In India, the total number of cold storage units, at present is 3443 was an installed capacity of around 10.3 million tonnes. Out of these 3443 cold storage units, 2975 are in the private sector, 303 in the cooperative sector and the rest in public sector (See Table 7.5). Out of

Table 7.5 : Cold Storage Industry in India

Year	Number	Storage Capacity (in million tonnes)
1947	4	0.003
1955	83	0.04
1960	359	0.31
1965	600	0.68
1970	1,218	1.64
1975	1,615	1.99
1980	2,283	3.96
1988	2,659	5.58
1990	2,930	7.68
1995	3,253	8.73
1999	3,443	10.30

Source : DMI Faridabad.

3443 nearly eighty-seven percentage of the cold storage units are operated by the private owners and having variable quality in refrigeration. Often not enough raw materials of good quality are available for food processing industry. Because of the existing warehousing facilities are very poor for agricultural and horticulture products in India. It is estimated that 13 to 15 per cent of agricultural products and more than 30 per cent of the horticultural products are lost due to lack of proper storage facilities. India wastes more fruits and vegetables than what is consumed in the whole of the U.K. Therefore, the non-availability of the hi-tech cold storage, nearly 40 per cent (Rs. 23000 crore) of the perishable products are spoiled.

Measures to Improve the Food Processing Industry

Even though the above factors act as non-incentive to the promotion of the food processing industry, there is immense scope for the growth of the food processing industry in India, provided the Government authorities and small scale entrepreneurs are taken into consideration the following aspects :

(i) Reducing the number of intermediaries in the food chain and identifying the source of raw material supplier and creating relationship with them in informal way.

(ii) The food processing industries should set up their own cold storage and transportation facilities. Installation of cold storage facilities according the production of vegetables and fruits should be undertaken at each production centre. Side by side efforts are also needed to promote the existing traditional storage methods in rural areas. Efforts are needed to start the mobile cold storage facilities in the growing areas.

(iii) It is advised to start the new food processing industry in the large scale manner so that they will provide quality goods consistently. The existing as well as new entrepreneurs in food industry should consider the local taste and preference and it will help to stabilize the business and also reap good amount of profit. The Indian consumer is sensitive to price changes.

Hence, prices will have to be kept under control and if possible it should be at lower level.

(iv) The task of teaching food processing and food marketing is presently not taken up by the Agricultural Universities and Hotel and Catering Technology Institutions. Hence, there is an urgent need for starting a Post-Graduate Course to impart the required knowledge, skill and confidence for efficient functioning of the food processing business units.

(v) The Government may further be released a number of food sectors like malt food, flour and milk food processing activities from the small scale sector reservation list.

(vi) To encourage foreign investment in the food and agricultural sectors of the economy, the Government has decided to give automatic clearance for joint venture with up to 40 per cent equity ownership by the foreign institutions.

(vii) The laws relating to food processing need to be updated and harmonized. The existing laws should be made more flexible to accommodate the changing situations like technological and marketing situations and consumer preferences. Further, there is urgent need to harmonize the food laws with international standards due to globalization.

(viii) The countries like Indonesia, Thailand, Philippines, Malaysia and U.S. do not impose any excise duty at all on food products. India too should avoid taxation on food products or at the very least.

Conclusions

The food processing industry has immense growth potential. The food processing sector can create not only more number of jobs but also provide immense opportunity for export. However, the growth of the industry can ultimately be rested with the hands of the Government and food processing industrialists. They work together to develop expertise and ideal business systems. The two can and should jointly identify the best practices and take necessary measures for the healthy development of the food processing industry.

References

A Correspondent, *Food Processing Immense Growth Potential,* The Hindu Survey on Indian Industries, 1988, pp. 18-23.

Anjali Shah, "Opportunities Unlimited", *Express Investment Week,* June 2-8, 1997, pp. 14-23.

Arun Sundaram,"Major Policy Incentives for Food Processing Industry", *The Economic Times,* 28th August 2000, p.14.

Economic Survey 1997-1998 and 1999-2000.

Paroda, R.S., *For a Food Secure Future,* The Hindu Survey on Indian Agriculture, 1999, p.18.

Satyasundaram, I. "Wheat: Problem of Plenty", *The Facts for You,* November 1999, pp.24-25.

Shashikant Hedge, "Investment in Food and Agro products immense scope", *The Economic Times,* 28th August, 2000, p.4.

Venkatesa, H.R., "Warehousing and processing: Means to bring industry status to agriculture and to make it profitable", *The Indian Journal of Commerce,* Vol. I, No.139, Part IV, December, 1997, p.126.

Vermudy, Vigneshwara, "Cold Storage of vegetables an unfinished task", *The Facts for You,* September 2000, pp. 25-28.

8

RICE MILL INDUSTRY : A Micro Level Study

— *S. Ramasamy* and *N. L. Tharani*

Introduction

Indian economy is basically an agricultural economy and agro-industries play a significant role in the country. Agro-industries process agricultural raw materials into final marketable products and their supply provide utility products to the consumers. Further, agro-processed wastes can also be used as fuel, fodder, fertilizer and fibre. The development of industries, particularly agro-industries, can promote agricultural development by creating forward and backward linkages. Agro-industrial activities add value to the farm products and directly generate additional employment opportunities and thus an increase in net farm income. This is true in the case of Rice Mill Industries which are functioning both in the rural and urban areas. The balance between agriculture and industries can bring prosperity and progress and help to achieve Mahatma Gandhi's dream, namely "Indians' prosperity lies in the development and progress of rural India". According to him "Rural India is real India", where agricultural activities provide livelihood for four out of five Indians.

Rice in the Indian Economy

Rice is one of the most important food crops in the world and the stapple diet for nearly half the world's population. Of the total consumption of cereals, one half is represented by rice. Rice though principally a tropical crop requiring high temperature and humidity for its growth, is cultivated both in the tropical and the sub-tropical zones of India, extending from 8° 5′ N to 27°N latitudes. Rice is grown under widely varying conditions of rainfall, altitude and climate. The paddy plant requires very hot and humid weather conditions and it requires a temperature of 15° C to 21° C during the sowing period, when it ripens. The temperature suitable vary from 30° C to 35° C. India is the second largest rice producer in the world. Production and marketing of rice is therefore India's foremost industry.

More than one-third of the national income is generated by agricultural sector and the rice mill industry also contributes considerably to our national income. Further, rice mill industry produced different by-products such as husk, bran, which are used as fuel, industrial furnaces, bedding material, insulation board and animal feed. There are two major cropping season in India: Kharif and Rabi. Rice is grown throughout the country but the principal production States are West Bengal, Andhra Pradesh, Tamil Nadu, Uttar Pradesh and Bihar. According to the Union Agricultural Ministry "Agricultural Statistics At A Glance 2000". West Bengal produces 15.5 per cent of the total rice in the country compared with 9.2 per cent in Punjab. The yield per hectare in paddy is highest in Tamil Nadu at 3,443 kg per hectare, whilst in Punjab, it is only 3152 kg per hectare. Close to West Bengal in rice production is Uttar Pradesh with 23.5 per cent and Andhra Pradesh with 13.3 per cent.

Rice Production

In the world, China is the single largest producer of rice and wheat in the world records with the average yield of 55 quintals against 31 quintals in India. The highest yield in the world is nearly 75 quintals (= 100kg) per hectare recorded in North Korea and Ireland. Rice is cultivated in about 45 million hectares of land, and rice covers the largest area among all the land under cereals. In terms of output, rice production is about 43 per cent of the output of all cereals.

In India, beginning 1951-52, when the First Five Year Plan was initiated, production was about 52 million tonnes. This was raised to 66.85 million tonnes in 1955-56, 138.41 million tonnes in 1987-88, and further to a high level of 203.0 million in 1998-99.

The total production of rice in India was 74.3 million tonnes in 1990-91 and it declined to 73.7 million tonnes in 1991-92. The decline in production was attributed to a decline in the area under cultivation of rice. Again in 1992-93, the rice production has declined to 72.6 million tonnes, due to decline in both area and yield. During 1993-94, rice production has exceeded the target of 78 million tonnes to reach 79 million tonnes, up by 6 million tonnes over the preceding year. Rice production has reached a record level of 81.8 million tonnes in 1994-95. However, production in 1995-96 came down to 76.6 million tonnes due to adverse weather and climatic conditions in Haryana, Punjab and Andhra Pradesh. The Economic Survey 1999-2000 exhibited has shown an estimated production of rice at 87.5 million tonnes in 1999-2000, which is 1.5 million tonnes higher than 1998-99 production of 86 million tonnes, despite heavy damage and to rice crop in Orissa (Table 8.1). Rice production in Tamil Nadu has increased from 6.6 million tonnes in 1991-92 to 8.2 million tonnes in 1998-99. Tamil Nadu's contribution to the total rice production in India has increased to 8.8 per cent during the same period (Table 8.2). This increase in production of rice both in India and Tamil Nadu was due to the increasing input of fertilizers and also with proper irrigation, contribution by major irrigation through canal system and minor irrigation through tube wells.

Rice Exports

Agricultural products which are presently being exported include rice, spices, tobacco, cashew, oilmeals and sesame, and ginger seeds,

Table 8.1 : Rice and Foodgrains Production in India

Commodity	Unit	1960-61	1970-71	1980-81	1990-91	1993-94	1994-95	1995-96	1996-97	1997-98	1998-99
Rice	Million Tonnes	34.6	42.2	53.6	74.3	80.3	81.8	77.0	81.7	82.5	86.0
Foodgrains	Million Tonnes	82	108.4	129.9	176.4	184.3	191.4	180.4	199.4	192.3	203.0
% Rice Production to Foodgrains Production	—	42.2	38.9	41.4	42.1	43.6	42.7	42.7	41	43	42.4
Area Under Rice	Million Hectares	34.1	37.6	40.1	42.7	42.8	42.8	42.8	43.4	43.4	44.6
Rice Yield Kg/ hectare		1013	1123	1336	1740	1888	1911	1797	1882	1900	1928

Source : Compiled from Government of India: *Economic Survey* 1992-93, 1996-97, 1997-98,1999-2000 (Ministry of Finance, New Delhi).

Table 8.2 : Foodgrain Production in India and Tamil Nadu

Particulars	1991-92	1992-93	1993-94	1994-95	1995-96	1996-97	1997-98	1998-99
Tamil Nadu	6.6	6.8	6.7	7.6	5.3	5.8	6.9	8.2
	(8.8)	(9.3)	(8.4)	(9.2)	(7)	(7.1)	(8.4)	(9.6)
India	74.7	72.9	80.3	81.8	76.9	81.7	82.5	85.9

Source : Compiled from Government of India, *Economic Survey* 1999-2000 (Ministry of Finance, New Delhi).

groundnut, spirit and beverages, guargum meal oil seed extractions, shellac, sugar and molasses, horticulture and horticulture products processed fruits and juices, meat and meat preparations.

Chronically, India had never been among the rice exporting nations until it attained self-sufficiency in rice production. Spectacular production and favourable buffer stock supply position coupled with growing demand for basmati rice in the international market, enabled India to export rice.

India's share of rice in the world exports was 0.6 per cent in 1970, and it rose to 3.7 per cent in 1980. In 1985, there was a tremendous decline in world exports and India's contribution has increased to 5.6 per cent in 1985. There was an increase in India's exports of rice to the world market by 6.4 per cent in 1990 and further increased to 12.6 per cent in 1997.

A Micro Level Study

With this background the researchers have made an attempt to study the RMI in Dindigul with the following objectives :

(a) To study status and economic structure of the rice mill industry,
(b) To examine the production process and energy use pattern in rice mill industry, and
(c) To find out the problems faced by rice mill industry and suggest the ways and means to solve the problems.

Profile of the study area

This study has been carried out in Dindigul. As per the records of the Rice Mill Owners' Association, there are 92 rice mill industries in Dindigul, of which 70 mills are functioning at present and the rest of them are defunct.

Methodology

The researchers have randomly chosen 35 rice mills and thus the sample selected constituted 50 per cent of the universe. A suitable interview schedule has been designed and pretested for the purpose of data collection. The interview schedule has been administered to the owners of rice mill industries. The interview schedule contained questions relating to general profile, sources of fund, capital structure, production process and production capacity details about machineries and equipments, employment, labour welfare measures, energy use pattern and problems faced by the rice mill industry. For the purpose of analysis, and percentages have been used wherever necessary. The major findings of the study are presented in Table 8.3 and 8.4.

Major Findings of the Study

* This study covered 35 RMI, of which 10 RMIs are ordinary mills (28.6 per cent) and 25 RMIs, are semi-modern mills (71.4 per cent).
* Out of the 35 RMIs 26 RMIs (74.0 per cent) and 9 RMIs (26.0 per cent) are operated under lease basis and ownership basis, respectively.
* The average size of a RMI in terms of total area, is 1.5 acres.
* In the RMI, the working capital constitutes 62 per cent and fixed capital constitutes 38 per cent.
* The average investment for a RMI is Rs. 0.885 million.
* The average monthly gross profit of a rice mill is Rs. 0.69 million.
* The average monthly energy consumption by a rice mill is 9723 kwh
* The total number of workers in the RMIs is 584 of which 54.45 per cent are female workers and 45.54 per cent male workers.
* Out of total input paddy used in the RMIs is 65.6 per cent of output in the form of rice, 11.5 per cent rice bran, 9.4 per cent paddy husk, 4.7 per cent broken rice and 8.7 per cent wastes and others.
* Among the total energy used in the rice mills, electricity constituted 52.4 per cent, paddy husk 38.14 per cent, groundnut shell 0.91 per cent and human energy 8.55 per cent.

Table 8.3 : Economic Characteristics of Rice Mill Industry

EB Capacity	No. of RMI Ordinary	Semi Modern	Total	Total Area (Sq.ft)	Total Capacity (Tonnes)	Capacity Utilisation %	Total No. of Labourers		Average Investment (Rs. Lakhs)	Average Profit (Rs. Lakhs)	Average Energy consumption (kwh)
							Male	Female			
< 25	2	0	2	49650	11745	7350 (64)	11	23	9.25	1.64	53.7
25-50	6	9	15	685610	114961	8707 (76)	113	123	4.7	12.08	7776.52
50-75	2	6	8	365482	63545	52540 (75)	61	70	8.70	0.91	6441.84
75-100	0	5	5	282850	51595	38675 (75)	44	48	14.8	8.08	7751.7
>100	0	5	5	36100	45747	36087 (79)	34	65	15.39	1.86	22515.3
Total	10	25	35	174962	287323	221739	266 (45.5)	318 (54.45)	8.85	6.90	9723.15
Average	—	—	—	4999	8209.23	6335.4	—	—	—	—	—

Note : S.P. — Sole Proprietorship P— Partnership, Sq. ft — Square feet, Tot— Total Figures in the parenthesis represents percentage.
Source : Computed from the primary data.

Table 8.4 : Annual Input (Paddy) and Output (Rice and By-products) of the Rice Mill Industry

EB Capacity	No.of RMI	Input Paddy Q	Rice Q	Rice bran Q	Rice Husk Q	Output Broken Rice Q	Others Q
< 25	2	2895.67 (100)	1930.45 (66.7)	347.48 (12)	289.56 (10)	144.80 (5)	483.7 (6.3)
25-50	15	29043.93 (100)	18913.79 (65)	3385.03 (11.65)	2604.87 (8.9)	1490.90 (5.1)	1715.9 (9.35)
50-75	8	14242.24 (100)	9687.88 (68.0)	1612.61 (11.3)	1366.63 (9.6)	674.70 (4.7)	900.4 (6.4)
75-100	5	11853.25 (100)	7574.24 (64)	1355.34 (11.4)	567.00 (4.7)	567.00 (4.7)	1227.22 (10.4)
>100	5	11054.76 (100)	7286.20 (66)	1297.02 (11.7)	1092.93 (9.9)	437.60 (4)	941.0 (8.4)
Total	35	69089.85 (100)	45392.56 (65.7)	7997.55 (11.5)	6483.44 (9.4)	3314.4 (4.7)	5902 (8.7)
Average	—	1974	1296.910	228.50	185.20	94.70	168.6

Note : Q— Quantity in tonnes. Figures in the Parentheses represent percentage.
Source : Computed from the primary data.

Problems and Solutions

(a) *Raw Material Problems*

* Inadequate finance to procure raw materials during harvest season.
* Seasonal variations in the price and the availability of input.
* Competition between different rice procedures during the time of procurement of paddy.
* Frequent and violent fluctuations of price of paddy.

Solutions

* Providing liberal, timely, adequate credit to the RMIs.
* Keeping adequate stock and procuring more paddy during bumper crops.
* Purchase of paddy in adequate quantity before increase in price.

(b) *Government Problems*

* Due to monopoly purchases of paddy by the Governmental, same ceiling limit is fixed by the Government.
* Frequent changes in the Government Policies in connection with RMI such as agricultural price policy (support price, procurement price and issue price).
* Unscrupulous ration rice sale in the open market at low prices that affect the sales volume of the RMIs.

Solutions

* Removal of monopoly purchase in certain areas and certain seasons and removal of ceiling limit during a particular season.
* Adopting flexible and liberal agricultural price policies.
* Adopting strict policy measures to control the sale of ration rice in the open market.

(c) *Labour Problems*

* Frequent demand for more wages by labourers who work in the RMIs.

* Difficulties in managing labourers.
* Inadequate labour availability during the busy seasons.
* Labour absenting from work without permission of RIM.

Solutions

* Offering eligible and minimum wages to the labourer. Persuading the labourers. Properly and keeping them in good mood through giving incentives during festivals and using affectionate words.
* Searching alternative labourers from other labour surplus areas by providing attractive incentives and wages.
* Changing labour if they absented from work without prior permission and giving them proper advise to them so as to inculcate the work ethics and work culture.

(d) *Machineries and Equipment Problems*

* Major and minor repairs of machinery and equipments occur during operation.

Solutions

* Major repairs could be solved by the mechanics.
* Minor repair by the drivers.
* Sometimes, equipments manufacturing companies may sent their mechanics to the RIMs.

(e) *Marketing Problems*

* Frequent and violent fluctuations of price of rice in the open market.
* Easy availability of poor quality rice at low price.
* Competition among different rice producers within and outside the State.
* Delay in receiving payments for rice already supplied to the wholesale dealers.

Solutions

* Maintaining sufficient rice stocks to avoid fluctuations in rice price.

- Regular supply of quality rice at reasonable price that attracts the consumers.
- Promoting customer service and thus avoiding competition between producers of rice, who may promote Rice Producers Federation.
- Restriction of credit sales and appointment of a person to look after the periodic dues collection from the wholesale dealers.

(f) Electricity Problem

- Frequent power cuts, low and high voltage problems in the area under the operation of RIMs.
- Sudden increase in electricity tariff, especially for industries, affects the profitability of the RIMs.

Solutions

- SEB can make an effort to control the high and low voltage problems.
- Introduce slow and steady increase in electricity traiff, for industrial sector.

(g) Direct Problems

- Low quality of paddy due to over use of chemical fertilizers in paddy production.
- Inadequate credit facilities for RIMs.

Solutions

- Advise the farmers to use the organic manure so as to increase the quality of paddy.
- Government should provide liberal, timely and adequate credit facilities to RIMs through various Financial Institutions.

(h) Indirect Problems

- Location of RIM influences the quantum of tax.
- Corruption among SEB's officials, labour welfare officers and municipalities.

Solutions

* Considerable reduction in the tax structure.
* Both the Government and people should cooperate to fight against corruption.

Conclusion

RMI is an agro-based industry providing direct and indirect employment, both in the rural and urban areas. The development of RMI depends upon agro-climate factors such as area under cultivation, cropping pattern, area under irrigation, and cultural factors such as food habits. Industrial environmental factors like Government support, policies such as agri-cultural price policy, energy policy, technological factors like machineries and equipments for RMI and above all human factors such as easy availability of labourers suitable for carrying out various production processes in the RMI. Further, it is concluded that the availability of energy is the most and important and vulnerable factors which the development of the RMI in a particular region.

References

Abhalakshmi Singi, *Agriculture and Rural Development,* B.R. Publishing Corporation, Delhi, 1998.

Bandyopadhyay, S. & Roy, N.C., *Rice Process Technology,* Oxford and IBH Publishing Co. Pvt. Ltd., New Delhi,1992.

Devendra Thakur, *Agro Based Industries,* Deep & Deep Publications, New Delhi,1998.

Government of India, *Economic Survey 1999-2000,* Ministry of Finance, New Delhi, 2000.

GRIAPPAS, *Prospects of Agro-Processing Industry,* Daya Publishing House, Delhi, 1996.

NEGLBS, *Agricultural Geography,* Kedar Nath Ram Nath, New Delhi.

Ruddardatt & Sundaram, K.P.M., *Indian Economy,* S. Chand, New Delhi,1999.

Sharma, Askok, B. "Grain Procurement Policy is based on Bad Economics", *Financial Express,* 23rd November, 2000.

Venkaian, V., *Impact of Agro-Based Industries on Rural Economy*, Himalaya Publishing House, Bombay,1997.

9

PROSPECTS AND PROBLEMS OF COIR INDUSTRY

— *M. Soundarapandian* and *S. Jagadees Pandi*

Introduction

Coir industry is one of the most traditional cottage industries concentrated in coconut producing States in the country. The only raw material required for the production of coir is coconut husk. The fibre extracted from the coconut husk is known as coir or coco fibre. Coconut grows ideally in humid tropics regions in India. The west coast belt regions accounts for more than 80 per cent of the area under this crop. Coconut cultivation and related activities offer employment to 3 million people. Being an export oriented industry it earns foreign exchange to the tune of 25 crores annually.

The coir industry mainly dispersed over the Western coast of Kerala, where the raw material is abundance. With an expansion of coconut cultivation coir industry is coming up in Tamil Nadu, Karnataka, Andhra Pradesh, Orissa, West Bengal. Kerala is the largest producer of coconuts contributing as much as 42 per cent of total production. Coir fibre is a versatile hard fibre used commercially for the manufacture of wide range of coir yarn, and products like mat and mattings, etc.

The coir industry is agro based and highly labour intensive, primarily due to the fact that such large number of *dalits* and economic weaker human beings depend for their life and happiness on the prosperity of the industry. It provides source of income about 5 lakhs artisans in rural areas. However, this industry has numerous problems, despite abundant availability of raw material, manpower natural facilities, transportations and infrastructural facilities, this industry could not make progress and it is a sad thing. Reasons are many and those reasons are traditional methods of production, illiteracy among the employees, lack of finance, marketing problems, high cost of raw materials and some political and sociological reasons have been responsible for slow and unsteady growth of coir industry in India. The present study attempts to analyse the prospects and constraints of coir industry in India.

The specific objectives of the study are :

* To study the growth and development of coir industry in India;
* To study the external markets performance of the coir industry;
* To review the problems faced by the Indian coir industry during the period;
* To study the concrete measures for raising the economic status of Coir Industry in India.

As far as the data is concerned secondary data is employed for the present study. The secondary data has been collected from annual reports of Coir Board, magazines etc. for the period of ten years from 1989 to 1999. The study have covered the production of coir and coir products, the market structure, export performance and the constraint of this industry.

Results and Discussions

Production of Coconut

The coir industry consists of two segments, namely white fibre and brown fibre . White fibre or retted fibre is extracted from husk of matured coconut after a process known as Rettings, which is more suited for spinning coir yarn, for further processing into finished products like door mats, mattings, carpets, geo textiles etc.

Brown fibre is extracted from coconut husk soaked in water for a number of days, by mechanical means. It is utilised for internal consumption for shifting upholstery manufacture of curled coir for rubberisation in the rubberised coir manufacturing industry, a part of the export too. Brown fibre is also used for producing ropes and finished products though on a limited scale only.

Development of coir industry depends on a largest extent of the availability of the basic raw material which is derived from the coconut. Therefore coconut is of great relevance and importance in the coir sector. The trend of area, production, productivity in India from the period 1989- 1998 is furnished in Table 9.1.

Table 9.1 : Area / Production / Productivity of Coconut in India

Year	Area ('000 ha)	Production (million nuts)	Productivity (nut/ha)
1989-90	1472.2	9358.5	6357
1990-91	1513.9	9700.2	6407
1991-92	5128.9	10079.6	6593
1992-93	1537.7	11240.9	7310
1993-94	1635.5	11974.7	7324
1994-95	1713.8	13299.6	7760
1995-96	1795.5	13967.9	7779
1996-97	1890.8	13061.8	6908
1997-98	1897.4	13088.8	6898

Source : Directorate of Economics & Statistics, Ministry of Agriculture.

The trend in the area under production of coconut as seen from the table that there was an increasing trend in the production on the coconut in India from 9358.5 million nuts in 1989-90 to 13967.9 million in 1995-96. But there was slow down from 1996-97 to 1997-98 due to some disease in coconut trees which are responsible for the decrease in production and productivity of coconut from

13061.8 million nuts during 1997- 98 to 13088.0 million nuts in 1997-98. The objective of the farming approach is to achieve a desired growth rate in the production and productivity of coconut at farm level. The major thrust shall be on soil and water conservation, recycling of used waters and developments of farming systems conducive to a steady increase in the output and income from the managed agro-eco systems.

Production of Coir in India

According to Coconut Development Board the annual production of coconut in 2001-2002 is estimated at 17,160 million nuts, of which 40 per cent would be used as tender coconuts leaving behind 60 per cent for industrial utilisation.

Production of coir products in India is estimated on the basis of actual exports, trends of internal consumption assessed from the movement of coir products by rail/streams/roads, and estimated consumption in the producing centres. The production of coir and coir products in India for the period of 1989-99 to 1998-99 is furnished in Table 9.2.

From Table 9.2 it is clear that the quantity of coir goods varied year after year. During the year 1989-90 the total production of white fibre is 1,25,900 tonnes and in 1998-99 is estimated at 12,400 tonnes, in-between 1989-90 to 1998-99 the quantity of white fibre remains the same. But when we look into the production of brown fibre, every year the quantity was increased. The quantity produced was 75,800 tonnes in 1989-90 and increased to 2,10,000 tonnes in 1998-99. The production of fibre is estimated in 2001-2002 at 3,74,000 tonnes. The production of white fibre is envisaged to decline to 75,000 tonnes from the current level of 1,27,000 tonnes. The growth in fibre production is expected only in the brown fibre sector. The production of coir yarn in 1989-90 was 1,15,400 tonnes and in 1998-99 is at 21,100 tonnes. Production of all products except white fibre increased year after year.

Under the plan programmes while persuing measures for advancement of white fibre. Coir sector coordinated action and concentrated efforts were made with the involvement of the

Table 9.2 : Production of Coir Products in India

ITEM s	1989-90	1990-91	1991-92	1992 -93	1993-94	1994-95	1995-96	1996-97	1997-98	1998-99
White Fibre	125900	126900	127000	127000	127000	127000	127000	127000	127000	124000
Brown Fibre	75800	84200	92600	101900	112100	123300	135600	149000	169000	210000
Coir Yarn	115400	131900	134500	143900	153900	164600	176200	185500	201000	211000
Coir Products	23490	24000	24700	25900	27300	40300	44000	48000	51500	58500
Coir Rope	39600	33300	34300	35300	36400	37500	38600	39800	39900	48000
Curled Coir	9000	14000	14700	16200	17800	21200	22000	24000	26000	28600
Rubberised Coir	15000	11100	12200	13400	14700	31500	33000	35000	37000	43000

Source : Data collected from Annual Report of Coir Industry, 1994-95 , 1998-99.

Industries Directorate of the government of the concerned State/ union territories and entrepreneurs whereas white coir production has remained stagnant due to non-availability of green husk in the required quantum.

Marketing of Coir Goods

The most important player in coir industry with reference to international trade is the exporters. There are two types of exporters in the coir industry, viz. (a) permanent exporters and (b) provisional registration holders. In the export market according to the Indian export destinations, about 67 countries all over the world import coir and coir products. Major Indian products are coir fibre, coir yarn mat and mattings, coirrugs, mourzouk, rubberised coir, coir geotextiles, coir poles, cocologs and coir pith. The major importing coir and coir products from India are USA, European countries, Canada, Australia, Russia etc.

USA is the single largest importer with the share of 19 per cent and EU countries put together import 68 per cent of the coir exported from India. With the globalisation and consequent liberalisation of trade policies a number of new exporters are entering the export trade in coir particularly on account of the present trend in favour of national products. Export of coir and coir products from India is presented in Table 9.3.

Table 9.3 : Export of Coir Products

Year	Quantity (In Tonnes)	Value (Rs in million)
1989-90	24958	401.75
1990-91	27428	483.28
1991-92	30999	741.18
1992-93	32354	959.53
1993-94	37951	1293.67
1994-95	48086	1716.40
1995-96	48276	2068.50
1996-97	46369	2125.80
1997-98	49850	2389.30
1998-99	55490	2921.90

Source : Coir Board, Cochin, 1999-2000.

From Table 9.4 it is clear that the beginning of 1990s witnessed an increasing trend in coir export. Export started picking up steadily and there was quantum jump in export from 27,526 tonnes during 1990-91 to 37,951 tonnes during 1993-94. The current year is still more encouraging and we have exported 55,490 tonnes during 1988-99. The target of export is fixed at 72,000 tonnes during 2001-2002 in quantum and Rs. 400 crore in the value of terminal year.

A major change that has happened in the Indian coir export is the change in Minimum Export Price Policy. With the process of globalisation and liberalisation of the Indian economy the Coir Board introduced MEP in 1996 to satisfy the requirement of Indian coir exports. The introduction of MEP ensured better export realisation to the exporters. The exporters took up the opportunity of excess production capacity bargain with the manufacturers to reduce the price. Under the new policy, embellishment has been taken out of the purview of MEP and also certain products like power loom products and geotextiles. The Indian coir products are in demand because of its special attributes, viz., (i) Fitness of purpose, (ii) price, (iii) craftsmanship, (iv) quality, (v) attractiveness.

Problems faced by the Coir Industry

The coir industry has stuck to traditional methods of production for historical and sociological reasons. The industry cannot go on far into the future, with its present method of production , mechanisation of defibring and spinning sectors would displace labour in large numbers. Inadequacy of raw material is one reason for the decrease in employment and the high cost raw material in the cost of production.

Primary coir is the large employer unit but mostly underemployment, part-time employment and secondary employment. With below par sustenance wages conditions of work to a large mass of unorganized casual workers. The entrepreneurial initiative in coir is essentially individualistic with a property orientation, even there are some corporate fecades. The role of professionalism is somewhat restrained by the very definition of trade structure large business houses of a country have chosen to keep away from coir and again, expatriate interest from consuming countries and multinational have been kept away.

The organisation of overall industry is fragile. The weakest link in its economic strength is a discarded waste husk becoming the primary raw material — lack of integration with the effective farming lobby of growers of coconuts — absence of large corporate and professionalism — absence of even remote nexus with product sector. These factors are inescapable realities not readily conducive for exponential forward in growth in volume: value, product profile and quality of coir industry.

The growth of coir in quantity or quality terms in its traditional settings is not optimistically promising while the economic disabilities of the commodities and the weakest of the trade and explicit coir areas, the social issues of the coir workers are compounding the complex problems.

When we take into account the market, the domestic market within the country largely by private traders. The internal consumption coir yarn in India is about 85 per cent and only 40 per cent of the indigenous production of coir door mat , mattings etc. is estimated to be consumed within the country.

Because of the emergence of plastic fibre, the substitute for fibre, the demand for coir fibre declining day by day. In spite of positive growth of coir products from India a general lowering trend has been noticed in the international market in the demand for coir products *vis-a-vis* other competing products. The reasons for this trend could be attributed to the ever increasing shift competition synthetic floor coverings and cheaper natural substitutes like gross products backed by aggressive marketing efforts. The marketing efforts of coir exporters is more or less confined to the age old conventional pattern and have not been very successful to create a niche for this product in the target market. It is a fact that the lack of overseas market intelligence especially for favourite designs, colours etc. and insufficient marketing efforts are serious impediments to increase coir exports. The traditional coir items such as coir mats, mattings, rugs carpets etc. have not shown appreciable growth of exports.

The high tariff rate for coir existing in various importing countries is one of the main hurdles for promoting coir and coir products. The tariff regime prevailing now varies between 2 to 30 per cent in various countries according to the information collected by the Coir Board. Apart from the tariff, very often several non-tariff barriers are impeding the growth of export market for coir products. They include allegations of child labour, restrictive banking facilities, import quota restriction, anti-dumping measures etc.

Suggestions

Though India has evolved several modern methods both in terms of product and marketing there are several potentials which we have not been able to tap. There are several countries where coir has not reached and several countries where coir products are available. The majority of the people do not know anything about coir. Coir and coir related products are definitely finding new applications and markets. However to succeed in these efforts, the industry has to be given emphasis to the following factors:

* Upgradation of the skill of workers through training for increasing productivity and income.
* Promotion of research and development in process improvement, product diversification, modernisation, elimination of drudgery and pollution and extension of fruits of R&D to the concerned sections in the coir industry.
* Improving the quality of coir yarn and coir products promoting new coir products like geo-textiles, rubberised coir, needed belt, coir pith etc.
* Development of new pattern of designs.
* Expansion of domestic market through market development scheme, participation in domestic exhibitions and fairs by Coir Board, publicity in T.V., newspapers etc.
* Increase in export through market development missions, sponsoring delegations participation in trade fairs and

exhibitions abroad.

* Congenial work atmosphere.

Conclusion

The liberalisation policy of the government is certainly a welcome thing and should be continued in the interest of the trade. It should be carried out more R&D work in the spinning areas of remote coastal belts to improve the method of production and also living conditions of coir workers. The raw material availability of coir industry, the coconut is available in abundance in India and further processing activities will generate employment to the village artisans engaged in this sector.

References

Agriculture and Industry Survey, Annual volume, Vadamalai Media, Coimbatore, 1997-98, pp. 237-242.

Coir Industry Current Status, Annual Report, Coir Board, Cochin, 1998-99, pp. 16.

Coir News, Coir Board, Cochin, vol. xxiv, January 96, pp. 17-22.

Coir News, Coir Board, vol. xxviii, December 99, Cochin, pp. 79-81.

Coir News, Coir Board, Cochin, vol. xxviii, July 99, pp. 19-25.

Coir News, Coir Board, Cochin, vol. xxviii, October 99, pp. 17-21.

10

COCONUT FIBRE UNITS IN TENKASI TALUK : A Case Study

— K. Thiripurasundari

This chapter attempts to analyse the working of the coconut fibre units in Tenkasi taluk. The chapter highlights the profile of the units, source of funds, profitability of the units, pattern of investment, area occupied, marketing of the fibre products etc.

In the Indian context, large scale industries cannot alone solve the problem of unemployment and underemployment. Mahatma Gandhi made a heroic effort to revive rural industries. He felt that they were a means of providing gainful employment.

Small Scale Industries play a vital role in the Indian economy. Today, the SSI (Small Scale Industry) sector produces almost 8000 products. The number of units has gone up from 19 lakhs in 1991 to over 31 lakhs in 1999. Perhaps, the most remarkable figures are in respect of employment. During the 7-year period from 1991 when liberalization began till 1998, the small scale sector created almost 42 lakh new jobs whereas the entire organised industry including Government was able to create only 14.3 lakh new jobs.

Industrial units though small can undoubtedly serve the economy in a big way. SSIs contributing 40 per cent of industrial production has in fact become a major thrust area in the industrial policies adopted.

Table 10.1 gives the overall performance of SSI sector.

Table 10.1 : Overall Performance of SSI Sector

Year	No.of Units (in lakhs)	Employment (in lakhs)	Production at current price (Rs. in crores)	Exports (Rs. in crores)
1991-92	20.82	129.80	178.699	13883
1992-93	22.46	134.06	209.300	17785
1993-94	23.84	139.38	241.648	25307
1994-95	25.71	146.56	293.031	38482
1995-96 (P)	27.24	152.61	356.213	36420 $

P - Provisional $ - Quick estimate
Source : Yojana, Vol. 39, No.13, November 1995, p. 13.

Considering the role played by the SSI units, our Government of India has taken important steps for their improvement. The Government of India has reserved about 900 items exclusively for production by small scale sector. Products of SSI are invariably given price and purchase preference support by way of supply of raw material and marketing assistance is extended to them. Financial assistance is also provided with low margins.

Thirunelveli district is one of the industrially backward districts of Tamil Nadu. Now this industrially backward district is slowly shedding its shuckler that hinders its industrial growth and a gradual transformation is taking place with several Medium and Small Scale Industries coming up with the liberalisation of the economy and the emphasis made on rapid industrialisation.

Tenkasi is one of the three revenue divisions of Tirunelveli district and also one among 11 taluks of the divisions. Tenkasi division is divided into 4 blocks, namely Shencottah, V.K. Pudur, Kadayanallur and Tenkasi block. The main occupation of the people of this area is agriculture. This area receives rainfall during both south-west and north-east monsoon seasons. The geographical features such as climate, rainfall and soil are well suited for growing coconut trees. Hence coconut cultivation is more in Tenkasi taluk. Since 1975, many coconut fibre units have been functioning in the Tenkasi taluk, with coconut husk as the raw material.

Fibre units are an agro-based industry. The units can be established everywhere mainly as it is a cottage industry and a SSI. These units have an excellent scope of broadening the economy.

Profile of the Fibre Units in Tenkasi Taluk

In the beginning stages, Tenkasi region supply coconuts to Tirunelveli and Madurai markets. Many small coconut merchants collect the coconut from the farmers of the area and stored them in their godowns. They peeled the coconut nuts and the husk as wastage. Later they supplied the husks to nearby brick kilns and in the tile factories, where husks are burnt to get fire.

At present Tenkasi taluk is dominated by fibre units. In southern zone 37 per cent of coconut cultivation was made by Tirunelveli District especially Tenkasi and Shengottai. Now 30 fibre units are functioning in Tenkasi as SSI.

Scope and Objectives of the Study

Since the researcher is familiar with the socio-economic conditions of Tenkasi taluk, the study was carried out. An attempt is made to study all the 30 fibre units. The scope of the study is limited to those fibre units functioning in Tenkasi taluk only and deals with the products like fibre, curled coir, rope, bio-organic manure and pith brick only.

The following are the objectives of the study :

1. To study the origin and growth of coconut fibre units in Tenkasi taluk.
2. To analyse the contribution made by the fibre units in Tenkasi taluk.
3. To study the wastage and its usefulness.
4. To study the factors which account for the drawbacks in these units.

Methodology

In order to fulfil the objectives set out, a field study was undertaken. This study was based on the responses obtained from 30 fibre units. The primary data for the study were collected through personal interview. A specially prepared interview schedule was used for collection of primary data. Primary data were supplemented by secondary data gathered from the municipal records and also technical books and journals.

In addition, data were collected from records of District Industrial Centre, Palayamkottai and Research and Extension Centre of Coir Board, Government of India, Tenkasi.

Analysis of Data

Both primary and secondary sources were used and for analysing several statistical tools were also used. Chi-square tests were used in appropriate places and according to the availability of data. Descriptive tables and percentage were also used for analysis.

The following pages were devoted for the analysis of the fibre units functioning in Tenkasi taluk.

Year of Establishment

The pioneer fibre unit was established in the year 1975 named 'Nellai Coir Unit'. An attempt is made to study the period of establishment of the units. The following Table 10.2 shows the period-wise establishment of the Units.

Table 10.2 : Year of Establishment

Year	No. of Units	Percentage
1975-80	1	3.33
1980-85	12	40.00
1985-90	10	33.33
1990-95	6	20.00
1995-2000	1	3.34
Total	30	100.00

Source : Primary data.

The table reveals the growth trend of fibre units in Tenkasi. Most of the fibre units were established during the 10-year period from 1980-1990. 40 per cent of the units were started during the 5-year period from 1980 to 1985.

Ownership Pattern

The ownership pattern of the fibre units shows that there exist four categories, namely — Sole proprietor, Partnership with relatives and with others and cooperative Society. The following Table 10.3 shows the ownership pattern.

Table 10.3 : Ownership Pattern

Sl. No.	Nature of Ownership	No. of Units	Percentage
1.	Sole Proprietorship	19	63.33
2.	Partnership with Relatives	6	20.00
3.	Partnership with Others	4	13.33
4.	Co-operative Society	1	3.34
Total		30	100.00

Source : Primary data.

It is learnt that the cooperative society is operated by Government. Majority of the units (63.33%) are in the nature of Sole Proprietorship. This is because, these type of Units require only small amount of investment. Moreover, the management of these units are very easy when compared to other SSIs. So the fibre units are dominated by sole proprietorship. Out of the 30 units, 10 units are in the nature of partnership.

Types of Products Manufactured

The 30 fibre units functioning in Tenkasi taluk produce mainly 3 types of products such as fibre, curled coir, pith manure and bricks. All the units informally produce rope for bundling the fibre.

In the initial years, fibre alone was produced. Later some development took place in these units and curled coir was produced as a by-product. Wastage of pith removal posed a problem to the entrepreneur. Hence to avoid that, bio-organic manure and bricks were produced by using the pith.

Table 10.4 : Type of Product and No. of Units

Sl. No.	Type of Product	No. of Units	Percentage
1.	Fibre	18	60.00
2.	Fibre and curled coir	10	33.33
3.	Fibre, curled coir and Pith manure & Bricks	2	6.67
		30	100.00

Source : Primary data.

The table shows that majority of units produce fibre only, i.e. 60 per cent. 33.33 per cent of the units namely 10 units produce fibre and curled coir. Bio-organic manure and bricks are recently developed during the years 1995 and 1999 respectively. Hence 6.67 per cent of units only involved in the utilization of pith.

Profitability of the Units

The following Table 10.5 shows the profitability position of the fibre units.

Table 10.5 : Profitability Position

Type of Units	% of profit
Fibre	29.25
Curled coir	37.5
Pith manure	46.67
Pith bricks	60.00

Source : Primary data.

The table shows that the units producing pith manure and pith bricks earn more profit than the other types of units. Those units produce fibre alone earn profit to the extent of 29.25 per cent only.

Sources of Funds

The sources from which the units raise their funds were given in the following Table 10.6.

Table 10.6 : Sources of Funds

Sources	Percentage of funds
Banks	40%
Friends and relatives	20%
Own capital	30%
Other sources	10%
Total	100%

The table shows that 40 per cent of funds was borrowed from banks like State Bank of India, Indian Overseas Bank, Indian Bank. 20 per cent of funds was borrowed from friends and relatives. 10 per cent was raised from Financial Institutions like DIC, IDBI, SIDBI etc. Majority of the funds were obtained only from banks, as loan.

Area Occupied

It is observed that out of the 30 units functioning in Tenkasi division, only 2 units have very big land of 8 to 12 acres including the land for coconut cultivation. 6 units have a land of 4 to 8 acres. It is learnt that for producing pith manure, bricks, fibre and curled coir, 4 acres of land is enough.

Hence an attempt is made to analyse the relationship between the area occupied by the units and the type of products produced by the units. Chi-square test is used for the analysis.

Hypothesis

There is no significant difference between the area occupied and type of product produced.

Table 10.7 : Area Occupied and Type of Product
Chi-Square test

Area in acre	Fibre	Fibre & curled coir	Fibre, curled coir and pith	Total	Percentage
1-4	15	6	1	22	73.33
4-8	2	3	1	6	20.00
8-12	1	1	—	2	6.67
Total	18	10	2	30	100.00

Calculated value of χ^2 = 1.43
Table value of χ^2 = 9.49

Since the calculated value is less than the table value, there is no significant difference between area occupied and type of products produced.

Investment Made by the Units

The investment pattern of the fibre units were studied. Generally it is learnt that the amount of investment made in the units differ with regard to the type of products produced. To produce fibre and curled coir, an investment of Rs. one to 15 lakhs were necessary which includes the cost of land and buildings. To make pith bricks and manure Rs. 20 lakhs are invested, because the cost of hydraulic machine is high. To have other facilities like transport, storage, drying process, an investment of Rs. 30 lakhs is necessary.

The following Table 10.8 shows the investment and type of unit.

Hypothesis

There is no significant difference between the amount of investment made and type of products produced.

Table 10.8 : Investment and Type of Product
Chi-square test

Investment (in lakhs)	Fibre	Fibre & curled coir	Fibre, curled coir and pith	Total	Percentage
1-15	14	5	—	19	63.33
15-30	3	3	2	8	26.67
Above 30	1	2	—	3	10.00
Total	18	10	2	30	100.00

Calculated value of χ^2 = 2.21
Table value of χ^2 = 9.49

There is no significant difference between the amount of investment made and the type of products produced, as the calculated value is less than the table value.

Marketing of Fibre Products

It is learnt that 17 fibre units market their products locally, 12 units market their products outside the State of Tamil Nadu. They market in the States of Kerala and Karnataka. Only 1 fibre unit exports its products to countries like Japan, U.S.A. and Korea. Hence, an attempt is made to analyse the relationship between the nature of the market and the type of products. The following Table 10.9 shows the position.

Hypothesis

There is no significant difference between the nature of market and type of products.

Table 10.9 : Marketing of Fibre Products
Chi-Squre test

Nature of market	Fibre	Fibre & Curled coir	Fibre, curled coir and pith	Total	%
Local	11	6	—	17	56.67
Outside the States	7	4	1	12	40.00
Outside the country	—	—	1	1	3.33
Total	18	10	2	30	100.00

Calculated value of χ^2 = 0.97
Table value of χ^2 = 9.49

The calculated value is less than the table value. So there is no significant difference between the nature of market and type of products.

Conclusion

The following are the findings of the study :

At present there are 30 fibre units functioning in Tenkasi taluk. All of them were declared as SSI under the Factories Act, 1948. All the units were registered in DIC and Coir Research and Extension Centre Board of India.

Most of the fibre units were established during the 10-year period ranging from 1980 to 1990.

Majority of the fibre units (19) were operated under sole proprietorship.

All the 30 units functioning in Tenkasi taluk produce mainly fibre, curled coir, pith manure and bricks.

Coconut husk is the raw material of these units. White fibre is produced from the green husk (fresh husk are used to produced brown fibre). Most of the fibre units produce 65 per cent brown fibre and 35 per cent white fibre.

From the husk, 20 per cent fibre only obtained and the remaining 80 per cent is pith. The fibre unit does not give any pollution problem because the pith is utilised for making bio-organic manure and pith bricks.

Compared to other coir products, pith brick product gives more profit, say 60 per cent.

The capital needed for starting fibre unit is about Rs. 1 to 15 lakhs. It will increase according to the size of the unit. Number of curling machine and other facilities such as storage, transport etc.

The financial assistance were provided by banks like State Bank of India, Indian Overseas Bank and Indian Bank 40 per cent of the funds requirements were met only these banks.

It was found out that for producing the fibre products, 4 acres of land is enough. Majority of the Units (22) have only 1 to 4 acres of land.

Most of the units (17) market their products locally. Only one unit exports its product to countries like Japan, USA and Korea. 12 units market their products to other neighbouring States like Kerala and Karnataka.

Chi-square tests were carried out to find out the relationship between different variables. The results of the tests are given below.

It was found that there is no significant difference between the area occupied by the units and type of products produced. There is no significant difference between the investment made and the type of products produced. It was also found that there is no significant difference between the nature of market and the type of product produced.

On the whole, it can be said that there were no major problems for the entrepreneurs regarding the availability of raw materials, marketing of products etc. However, some of the entrepreneurs were of the view that they face difficulties in getting sufficient funds. Lesser amount of subsidy, higher electricity charges were some of their problems. Summer season (January-May) is the best suited season for the fibre units, but usually there is the water scarcity during this season. So water scarcity is another problem for the units.

Hence, it can be concluded that the core business is the lucrative business in Tenkasi taluk. If Coir Board takes necessary steps to solve their problems, then the coir business will progress in the years to come.

References

Bose, T.K., *Fruits of India — Tropical and Subtropical,* Calcutta, Nayaraprakash, 1985.

Journal : Coir News, Aug., Sept. and Oct. Issues, Ernakulam.

Khan, R.R., *Management of Small Scale Industries,* New Delhi, Sultan Chand, 1979.

Patel, J.S., *The Coconut,* Madras, Wiley Eultern Ltd., 1938.

Sadasivam, S. and Manicam, A., *Bio-Chemical Methods for Agricultural Science,* Madras, Government, Press, 1996.

Sankaran, S., *Agriculture Economy of India,* Madras, 1979.

11

WOMEN IN DAIRY INDUSTRY : A Study in Dindigul District

— *M. Soundarapandian* and *N. Siva Kumar*

Introduction

India occupies third place in the dairy industry followed by USSR and USA. India's milk production in 1995-96 was 70.8 million tonnes. Thus the dairy industry in India has now come to occupy a place of pride in the national economic scene. Dairy has special significance for women's employment, as an important subsidiary occupation in order to enhance the family income and to reduce pressure on crop production in rural area. The point in favour of women in dairy is that, there is greater degree of indoor activities in dairying. The fact remains that today agriculture has been becoming increasingly a female activity.

Between 1971-81, the ratio of female to male agriculture labour went up from 51 to 60 per cent. The ratio of female to male cultivators also rose from 14 to 19 per cent. Tamil Nadu and Karnataka between 40 and 60 per cent of agricultural work done by women. Thus rural India is witnessing an intraining process described as "FEMINISATION OF AGRICULTURE". In order to provide opportunities to rural women to improve their lot by taking up economic activities, it is necessary to organise them by identifying various sectors where their involvement has been more. Share of employment in the rural unorganised sector as held by women, can be traced to the major employment systems. These are: agriculture, dairy, animal husbandry, fisheries, social and agro-forestry, khadi and village industries, handlooms, handicrafts and sericulture out of these employment system, women's involvement has been found to be intensive in dairy and animal husbandry activities.

However such involvement of women is mostly in the non-market sector, usually intermittently in combination with many other farm tasks. The present study is an attempt to find the women participation in dairy industry. The specific objectives of the study are:

* To study the participation of women in dairy operation.
* To asses the knowledge level of women dairy farmers regarding scientific practices.
* To investigate impact of dairying on women income

The study is descriptive one based on survey method. Nilakottai Block in Dindigul district has been purposively selected as the area of the present study. Cooperative Society and Rashtriya Mahila Kosh Scheme implemented by ASSEFA constitute the respondence of the study. The women who are the member of Pallapatty milk cooperative society and RMK schemes form the respondents. Based on non-proportionate random sampling, 50 members each from co-operative society and RMK scheme implemented by ASSEFA were selected.

The study is based on both primary and secondary data. The secondary data were collected from Pallapatty milk society and RMK records. The primary data related to socio-economic conditions of women dairy farmers, the knowledge level regarding scientific dairy practices, activities performed by women, profit realised by women through dairying and control of women over the profit were collected from selected respondents.

Two interview schedules, bearing on the objectives, of the study were prepared. The first schedule collected information from Secretary of Pallapatty Milk Co-operative Society and Branch Manager of RMK. The second schedule aimed at collecting data from dairy women in this study area. Conventional tools like average and percentage have been used for analysing the data.

Result and Discussion

Dairy industry has turned in an impressive performance. It has developed not as a secondary occupation but as a main occupation with several people depending entirely on dairy. In Tamil Nadu, the total membership of women in dairy cooperatives is 27.1 per cent, in Himachal Pradesh 17.77 per cent, in Gujarat 5.0 per cent and in Bihar 11.3 per cent.

Socio-Economic Condition

The majority of the women beneficiaries of co-operative society belong to the age group of 20-40 mostly illiterates and belongs to backward class community. Nature of house is also mostly hutment type. Nuclear family type is highest. Agricultural coolies are mostly doing dairy business.

Breeds of Animals

The productivity of milch animals are highly influenced by breed character of the stock. Hence, efforts are initiated to popularise high yielding (Cross-breed cows and graded). Though cross breeding of the indigenous breeds of cows with exotic breeds and local breeds. The advantages of artificial insemination, efforts were initiated to adopt this technique towards genetic improvements and breed developments of milch animals.

Table 11.1 : Breeds of Animals

Sl. No.	Name of the Breed	Co-op. Group member %	RMK group member %
1.	Non-descriptive	6%	—
2.	Cross breed	94%	100%
3.	Graded	—	—

Source : Computed from primary data.

Table 11.1 reveals that the breeds of the animal. The respondents possess only 6 per cent of co-operative society members have got non-descriptive breed milch animals. About 94 per cent and cent per cent of co-operative society women members and RMK group women members respectively have got cross bred variety and none of the respondents possess a graded milch animal.

In most of the co-operative society women member having only one animal. But most of the RMK group women members having three and above animals.

Availability of Grazing Land

The population pressure and its impact on the land-use pattern, the land available for grazing has been declining in Tamil Nadu. Moreover, due to overgrazing and other reasons the quality of the existing grazing land would have also declined. These aspects would have led to reduction in the dependence on grazing and a shift in the feeding practice from grazing to stall feeding.

Table 11.2 : Availability of Grazing land

Sl. No.	Particulars	Co-op. Group member Member %	RMK group %
1.	With grazing land	34%	24%
2.	Without grazing land	66%	76%

Source : Computed from primary data.

Table 11.2 shows that availability of grazing land for the respondent are 34 per cent of co-operative society members and 24 per cent of RMK members having grazing land. The milch animals stallfed totally or stallfed and grazed the provided with various combinations of feed inputs. Though the feed inputs are of various verieties, forms and nutrient content, they can be broadly divided into two, namely, roughages and concentrates. Roughages are bulked feeds containing high percentage of fibre content and low indigestible nutrient concentrates are low fibre and high in total digestible nutrients.

Awareness of Women about Cattle Rearing Technology

Cattle rearing technology is expected to improve productivity and production and also to reduce cost of production. However, as technological change is costlier, it is generally class-biased in nature. In this context, we shall highlight the awareness to women about cattle rearing technology.

Table 11.3 reveals that levels of women are aware in cattle rearing management and technology. All the respondents in co-operative society 96 per cent of the respondents in RMK group members are aware about artificial insemination. About 54 per cent and 28 per cent in co-operative society members and RMK group members respectively are aware about frozen semen. About 88 per cent and 96 per cent from co-operative society members and RMK group members respectively are aware about heat symptoms.

Table 11.3 : Awareness of Women about Cattle Rearing Technology

Sl. No.	Particulars	Co-op. Group member %	RMK group Member %
1.	Artificial Immunisation	100%	96%
2.	Frozen semen	54%	28%
3.	Heat symptoms	88%	96%
4.	Deworming	14%	24%
5.	Dehorning	4%	—
6.	Weaning	74%	84%

Source : Computed from Primary data.

Only 14 per cent from co-operative society members and 24 per cent from RMK members are aware of deworming. Only 4 per cent from co-operative society members are aware of Dehorning and 74 per cent and 84 per cent from co-operative society members and RMK group member respectively are aware of weaning of the cattle.

Due to the fact that the artificial insemination is better than natural insemination on the almost all the respondents are aware of artificial insemination. The use of forzen semen is a new technological concept, so the respondents awareness about it is low. It is clearly observed that there is very little awareness about the advantage of Dehorning as only 4 percentage of the members of co-operative society practice this in their cattle. The practice of deworming is also less and it can be inferred that there is not much awareness about this too.

Decision Making Process of Dairy Practice

During the last fifty years Indian dairy industry has grown from almost unorganised sector to a vastly complex industry of a large magnitude with the formation of dairy cooperative societies. Women are generally associated with animal husbandry activities which are performed at house and they spend longer hours than men in dairying activities.

Table 11.4 : Decision making process of Dairy practice

Sl. No.	Particulars	Co-operative Society members			RMK Group members		
		Male	Female	Both	Male	Female	Both
1.	Animal Purchasing	90%	4%	6%	62%	26%	12%
2.	Feed Purchasing Animal	10%	76%	14%	22 %	34%	44%
3.	Animal Breeding	16%	72%	12%	26%	54%	20%
4.	Fodder Purchasing	34%	46%	20%	28%	56%	16%
5.	Milk Marketing	22%	66%	12%	34%	54%	12%
6.	Family Expenses	28%	24%	48%	14%	36%	50%

Source : Computed from primary data.

Economic Analysis of Women Dairy Farm

Poverty and unemployment rates followed by the glaring inequalities of income and consumption have been substantial. The animal production enterprises particularly dairying provide not only much larger additional employment opportunities to rural women. Dairy industry provides off- season work steady income and keeps the women employed all the year round. In certain areas, it has been obscured that as much as fifty per cent of the income, derived by rural households is from dairying alone.

Table 11.5 : Economics of one cow unit

Sl. No.	Details	Co-operative Society Group Members	RMK Group Members
A.	FIXED COST		
1.	Average cost of milch cow	8,000	7,500
2.	Building cost	1,000	1,000
3.	Equipments		
	(a) Depreciation cost of animal at the rate of 10 per cent of the total value of cow	800	750
	(b) Depreciation cost of building at the rate of 5 per cent of the total value	50	50
	(c) Depreciation cost of equipment at the rate of 10 per cent of the total value of the equipment	50	50
B.	RECURRING COST		
1.	Cost of dry fodder	2,555	3,650
2.	Cost of green fodder	1,460	1,825
3.	Concentrate feeding	3,650	3,650
4.	Insurance 5 per cent of the total value of the animal	400	360
5.	Veterinary medicine	200	200
	Total cost	8,265	9,635
	Total fixed cost + Total recurring cost	9,165	10,485

Sl. No.	Details	Co-operative Society Group Members	RMK Group Members
C.	**INCOME**		
1.	Sale of milk	17,520 (2190 Lr @Rs.8)	20,162 (2372.5 Lr @ 8.5)
2.	Sale of Manure	500	600
	Total income	18,020	20,762
3.	Net profit	8,855	10,277

Source : Computed from primary data.

Table 11.5 reveals that the economies of one cow unit run by the women under the two different groups, namely co-operative society members and RMK group members. The average cost of one milch cow of co-operative society members and RMK members is 8,000 and 7,500 respectively. Building cost of co-operative society members and RMK members is each 1,000. The cot of dry fodder of co-operative society member and RMK member is 2,555 and 2,650 respectively. The cost of green fodder of co-operative society members and RMK members is 1,460 and 1,825 respectively. The cost of concentrated feeding of co-operative society members and RMK group members is 400 and 360 respectively. The veterinary medicine cost is also 200 and 150 respectively. It is obvious from the income statement that sale of milk for Rs. 17,520 for co-operative society members and Rs. 20,162 for RMK group members. Sale of manure is for Rs. 500 and Rs. 600 for co-operative society members and RMK group members respectively. The total income for co-operative society members and RMK members is Rs. 18,020 and Rs. 20,762 respectively. The net profit for co-operative society members and RMK members is Rs. 18,020 and Rs. 20,762 respectively. The net profit for co-operative society members is observed to Rs. 8,855 and RMK group members is 10,277. It is clear that the income of RMK group members is higher than that of co-operative society members is due to reason that the organisers of RMK group visit the members regularly and conduct programme regularly.

Suggestions

* As most of the co-operative society member and RMK group members are illiterate, it is suggested that steps should be taken to educate them by which they will be able to understand the proper animal rearing methods.
* Dairy farming assumes a greater importance as it remains one of the allied activities of agriculture and it is reliable source of income too. Hence, an awareness should be created among women about the scientific techniques to dairy farming.
* Measures can be taken to maintain community grazing land with different kinds of fodder crops like perennial fodder crops like BN2, CO1,CO2, CO3 and Fodder trees subabul, agathi and Glyrieidia along the bunds.
* Dry fodder should be supplied in veterinary centre at controlled rates.
* Cost incurred towards feeds and fodder can be minimized by preparing and feeding optimal combination of feeds and fodders.
* To improve and ensure the production of clean milk, sufficient educative measures must be undertaken.
* The co-operative milk society or RMK should also launch continuous educational programmes on a massive scale to improve skill and competence to milk producers. The technique of better management of quality animals.
* Demonstration have to be undertaken frequently for farmers to have adequate knowledge about dairying.
* Camps and training can be arranged for women to disseminate knowledge on breeding technology, vaccine and disease control, fodder production technology, the use of deworming, Dehorning, etc.
* Opening of more veterinary dispensaries and sub-centre are necessary for their timely assistance.
* Opinion of women must be taken into consideration so that women improve their leadership qualities and become efficient decision makers.

* Each and every women must be educated on dairy farming in a way that she is capable of managing her activity profitably.

Conclusion

In the fast moving world of ours, particularly in a country like India, one forgets and does not care to stop for a while and have a look at rural women who are poor in their personal as well as societal life. They are very low in their economic status and their opinions and views are not given much importance. It is a common understanding that people in the rural areas are engaged in agriculture. Dairy farming is an allied activity of agriculture which views an added income to those involved in agriculture. In order to learn the part played by dairy farming in the lives of rural people, in the present study, the role of women folk in dairy farming has been studied, making a comparison between co-operative society members and RMK group members. RMK beneficiaries are able to get more profit compared to women beneficiaries of co-operatives as majority of them own three milch animals Moreover, working capital to meet the maintenance expenditure is not problem to them; as the women of RMK rotate their savings amount and get frequent loan. Thus the study reveals that women beneficiaries of RMK fare better than milk co-operatives as they are better organised under self-help group scheme.

References

Banerjee, G.C., *A Text Book of Animal Husbandry,* Seventh Edition, Oxford and IBH Publishing Co. Pvt. Ltd., New Delhi, 1995.

Chotani, A.A., *A Model for Dairy Co-operative,* National Dairy Development Board, Anand, Gujarat, 1975.

Das, S.K., "Impact of Dairying on Indian Economy", *Dairy Guide,* September 1990.

Gopalakrishnan, C.A., *Livestock and Poultry Enterprises for Rural Development,* Vikas Publishing Company, Pvt. Ltd., New Delhi, 1985.

Kulandaisamy, V., *Co-operative Dairying in India,* Rainbow Publications, Coimbatore, 1986.

Mishra, G.P., *Impact of Dairy Development in Rural Areas of Karnataka,* Institute for Social and Economic Change, Bangalore, 1979.

Pitchai, Dairy Co-operative for Rural Development, *Tamil Nadu Journal of Co-operation,* February 1991.

Subha, Promising Fodder to Dairy Industry, *Tamil Nadu Journal of Co-operation,* June 1991.

12

EMERGING CHALLENGES IN DAIRY INDUSTRY

— *M. Seethalakshmi* and *N. Lalitha*

Introduction

In the emerging liberalized global scenario, the heavy subsidies prevalent in the dairy sector, in the countries of European Union as well as United States have been brought down, resulting in substantial competitive advantage to India. Indian dairy industry with substantial investment can emerge as a major exporter of dairy products. It is imperative to evolve a long-term dairy industry policy that will not only sustain, but also enhance production and productivity levels.

For sheer numbers, India's dairying has no match in the world about 70 million farmers, maintaining a milch herd of little under 100 million — 57 million cows and 39 million buffaloes. Fed largely on crop residues their milk yield in 1997 was estimated at 74.3 million tonnes.[1]

Constraints

Dairy industry in India encounters with some constraints, which include the following :

1. Per capita availability of milk stands at 214 gm/day as against 300 gm/day as recommended by Indian Council of Medical Research (ICMR).
2. Though Indian dairying had made rapid strides the animal productivity remains low, averaging 1.5 litres/day.

Table 12.1 : Trends in the Production of Milk Per Capita Availability and Human Population — India

Items	Milk in tonnes	Per capita availability in gms/day	Human population in millions
1950-51	17.0	132	361.1
1960-61	20.0	127	439.2
1970-71	22.0	112	548.2
1980-81	31.6	131	685.3
1985-86	44.0	162	763.2
1990-91	53.7	181	831.1
1994-95	63.3	199	923.2
1996-97	74.3	214	953.0

Source : Dairy India - 1997.

3. Though milk is an essential nutrients wholesale food, providing 95 per cent of animal proteins and almost 100 per cent of animal fat in the dairy diet, low parchasing power of the vast majority of people depresses the demand for milk — the food for excellence. Thus notwithstanding the limitations given above Indian dairy sector has vibrant future. Burgeoning income across all sections of the urban population has given a spurt demand for milk. All income groups in urban and rural areas reported higher expenditure of milk, according to the findings of the consumer survey conducted by the National Sample Survey Organization (NSSO)[2], Government of India.

Besides this increase in demand for milk within the country India has to tap the export opportunity provided by WTO through the opening of protected market and reduction in subsidies. The Asian dairy market for milk products may not be the world's biggest but they are the world's fastest growing market. India with some 27 per cent of Asian's population accounts for more than half of the milk output in this vast continent. The consumption of milk and milk products has grown rapidly among the affluent by 3 million tonnes[3] per year. They are following the path of Japan where milk consumption has more than trebled to 70 kg per capita today from a mere 20 kg in the 'sixties'. This presents excellent opportunity for India to meet part of the spiralling demand of the countries in East and South-East Asia. Two countries, which do not subsidise their dairy farmers, are New Zealand and India. To protect domestic markets, heavy restrictions were placed on competitive imports. These protective policies are now undergoing a sea-change under the impact of GATT agreement 1993, being implemented through the new World Trade Organisations (WTO) created in 1995.

Described as the greatest and most comprehensive trade agreement into world history, GATT heralds a new era of free trade through the opening of protected markets and sharp reduction of exports subsidies. It is expected to produce a big shakeup in the dairy industry in Europe, North America and Australia. For India, it can be a blessing in disguise, facilitating the country's presence in the world dairy trade. After producer's subsidies are reduced in major exporting countries, Indian diary products will become price competitive. Another favourable factor for India is the geographical location in the proximity of major dairy markets.

The Asia-Pacific region will remain a net milk importer in the future. These countries accounts for the bulk of milk powder imports and half of the imports of condensed and evaporated milk (Tables 12.2 and 12.3).

Another significant world market is emerging from Russia to world's biggest dairy importer and this situation will continue for next 20 years. Although by far the biggest milk producer in Europe, the Russian output has declined by more than 25 per cent in the past five years. The shortfall in production is estimated to be 13 million tonnes a year. Their major deficits in milk availability offer a rare opportunity for India to fill this vacuum to take its place among leading dairy exporting nations.

Table 12.2 : Dairy product imports in Asia-Pacific region's developing countries, 1986 and 1991

Country	1986 Value	1991			
		Value	Growth over 1986	Milk (liquid eq.) ('000 tonnes)	Percentage of locally produced milk
Bangladesh	62088	91050	46.6	313	80.5
China	219484	355977	62.2	1010	88.2
Fiji	6174	7638	23.7	22	73.8
Indonesia	56320	99543	76.7	405	68.3
Iran	136975	211440	54.3	930	77.6
Malaysia	95387	203896	113.7	968	4.5
Myanmar	5250	4880	-0.07	9	98.3
Nepal	3700	4128	11.5	5	99.5
Pakistan	29460	31120	5.6	179	99.2
Papua NG	7750	14440	86.3	30	—
Philippines	106817	242000	126.7	1200	2.8
Singapore	88433	187208	111.7	NA	NA
South Korea	8223	42582	417.8	155	92.4
Sri Lanka	32058	65769	105.1	357	37.8
Thailand	79832	157987	97.9	638	23.7
Vietnam	5300	7000	32.0	14	82.5
Sub-total	943251	11726658	99.0	6212	0.0
Others	34147	16389	1.0	23	NA
Total	977398	174307	78.3	6.235	3.7
World	13884329	21177449			

Source : Dairy India, 1997.

Table 12.3 shows the India's exports and imports of milk and milk products between 1992-95.

It is observed from the table exports are picking up, having gone up by 40 per cent of value, in the first half of the 90s and to an estimated rupees 400 millions by 1994-95. A significant contribution is made by Gujarat the Cooperative Milk Marketing Federation Ltd., which is the largest exporter of dairy products valued at Rs.18.3 crores in 1995-96.

The three-fold challenges before the Indian dairy industry lies

Table 12.3 : India's export and import of milk products, 1992-95

	Exports						Imports					
	1992-93		1993-94		1994-95		1992-93		1993-94		1994-95	
	Qty.	Value	Qty.	Value	Qty.	Value	Qty.	Value	Qty.	Value	Qty.	Value
Ghee	479.3	446.7	375.2	331.3	613.1	642.3	—	—	—	—	—	—
SMP	80.1	51.6	671.8	263.5	5947.6	2178.7	7133	4152.8	2198.7	1381.2	215.1	158.1
VMP	101.2	74.1	161.5	79.0	1161.6	444.2	—	—	—	—	—	—
Baby food	394.6	242.8	203.6	133.1	25.6	16.9	64.5	70.2	57.5	66.7	9.1	7.6
Butter oil	—	—	—	—	—	—	569.7	353.8	122.6	73.1	4389.2	2462.2

Sources : Agricultural & Processed Food Products Export Development Authority (ADEDA), New Delhi.
Dairy India 1997.

in quality improvement, product development and marketing. It calls for substantial efforts towards professional management in dairy industry with updated knowledge for dairy technologies and professional skills for the dairy milk producers.

Export opportunities are knocking at the door of dairy industry. To meet the emerging challenges, by meeting the international standards dairy management should be professionalised. Our planners took timely and corrective measure to meet the sanitary and phyto-sanitary specifications, as prescribed by Office International des Epizooties (OIE) under the World Trade Organisation. These specifications are also extended to the health states of cattle and livestock. Consequently the main thrust of the Ninth Plan proposal is on the improvement of animal health and adoption of sanitation and phyto-sanitary specifications for dairy products, i.e. 28.1 per cent for health out of the total outlay of Rs.1965 crores.

Table 12.4 : Ninth Plan outlay for AH & D activities

	Amount (Rs. crores)	%
Animal health	552	28.1
Dairy development	485	24.6
Meat % meat products	396	20.2
Cattle development	151	7.7
AH Statistics	126	6.4
Fodder development	90	4.5
Poultry	90	4.5
Sheep, goat, rabbit	75	4.0
	1965	100.0

Conclusion

The Indian dairy industry is gearing itself to face new challenges and opportunities ir the 21st Century. Its strength lies in the synergistic partnership forged between the farmer and dairy professional, combining the farmers traditional wisdom and the energy with latter's knowledge and skill. This will impart confidence and strength to India's white revolution, giving it direction and necessary thrust. All segments of the industry must be together in a partnership to spark the next miracle in the emergence of India as the world's leading dairy nations not merely becoming the biggest but also the best.

References

Dairy India, 1997.

Ganesh Kumar, B., and R. Prabhakaran, (2000), Dairying in India (thrust for 21st Century), *Indian Economic Panorama,* Vol. 9, No. 4, pp. 18-21.

Vasanth, P. Gandhi *et.al,* (1995), "Growing importance of milk — in food expenditure", *Indian Journal of Agricultural Economics.*

13

PROBLEMS OF MILK PRODUCTION AMONG MILK PRODUCERS

— *M. Sivasubramanian* and *C. Madhavi*

Introduction

Dairy development in India is recognized as an effective instrument for ameliorating the economic conditions of rural families, particularly those of the small and marginal farmers and the landless agricultural labourers. The reduction of rural poverty and income inequality have been principal and paramount objectives of agricultural development in India. However, growth in agriculture alone cannot be sufficient to bring about a substantial reduction in income inequality and poverty. Therefore, reliance on dairy sector has also become an inevitable process in Indian economy.

There is a close relationship between agriculture and dairy sector in India. Dairy sector enables farmers to generate the working capital to produce the needed input for agriculture, such as seeds, fertilizers, pesticides etc. In rural areas, owning of milch animals contributes not only to the dairy industry, but also to agriculture by way of providing manure, dung fuel, feed wastages and animal labour. In the total output of dairy animal milk accounts for 64.5 per cent and the rest 35.5 per cent comes from cattle manure, hides and meat.

Milk production can be considered as a yardstick to assess the growth of dairying in any country. In order to link the dairy development with rural development programmes, the government has introduced milk producers' co-operative societies at various levels. The main objectives of milk producers' co-operative societies are to safeguard and protect the interest of milk producers organize marketing facilities for their members and fetch remunerative price for milk. Being responsive to the milk producers' these societies are expected to provide the inputs like, fodder seeds, artificial insemination and veterinary facility to augment milk production.

Most of the milk is produced in rural areas. In village, the bulk of milk trade is controlled by small private traders who purchase milk from rural milk producers and transport it by bicycle and other modes of transport to nearby towns to sell it. There are also private small time operations who purchase milk from the milk producers to convert it into milk products. The price offered by these traders is determined by the marketable surplus of milk and the demand for milk. However, the seasonal increase in milk production leads to decrease in the price offered to milk producers during flush season.

Milk marketing is determined by the level of production and in this connection, a few village level research studies are undertaken to analyze factors which influence the milk production with respect to selected farm households of various categories drawn from to high potential areas and low potential areas to make the validity of empirical validation of the present study.

It is observed that researcher in management discipline have given much priority and weightage to analyze the problems and prospects of business and industrial activities but it is noticed that rural development has received less attention. In India more than 76 per cent of people are living in nearly 6,27,000 villages. The development of India depends on the development of villages mainly in the growth of agriculture and its allied activities like the dairy sector, which provides livelihood to the majority of the population either directly or indirectly. Hence, the management of rural development should be given due weightage. Recently, the management personnel have realised much of its importance in achieving in this academic field. In order to fulfil this gap, the present study has been undertaken.

The specific objectives of the study are :

1. To examine the factors influencing milk production among the different categories of milk producers.
2. To compare the level of milk production among the milk producers.

The analysis relates to an appraisal of milk production capacity and its correlated factors and dependent factors from the point of view of milk producers selected from the four villages. Though the present study aims to investigate the milk production in Tamil Nadu, field investigation has been confined to four villages selected from two villages in each district (Salem and South Arcot) in Tamil Nadu to collect the data from the producer's point of view. The investigator has adopted the method of multistage random sampling to collect the needed data from producer's point of view. In the selection of districts, a high potential district (Salem district) and a low potential district (South Arcot district) in milk production from the groups of high potential and low potential districts in the State were selected.

Results and Discussion

Table 13.1 presents data on milk yield per animal in the different regions. It could be seen that Salem district's high potential village rank first in order of milk yield per animal per day as it records 6.01 litres and the same district low potential village comes next in order. South Arcot districts high potential village occupied the third position with 4.97 litres and the same district's low potential village is placed in the last position.

It could be seen from the above discussion that the milk productivity per animal in low potential village of Salem district is even greater than high potential village of South Arcot district.

Table 13.1 : Milk Yield per Animal — Region

Region	High Potential district		Low Potential district		Total Average
	High Potential Village	Low Potential Village	High Potential Village	Low Potential Village	
Milk Yield (in litres)	6.01	5.87	4.97	4.67	5.38

Data presented in Table 13.2 indicates the herdsizewise milk yield per animal per day. It is seen that small herdsize group ranks first in order of milk yield as it is worked out to 5.72 litres. The medium herdsize group comes next in order as it records 5.55 litres of milk. The large herdsize group stands last in milk yield as it worked out to 4.53 litres.

Table 13.2 : Milk Yield per Animal — Herdsize

Herdsize	Small	Medium	Large	Total Average
Milk Yield (in litres)	5.72	5.55	4.53	5.38

It could be deduced from the above interpretation that milk yield is remarkable high among the small herdsize respondents indicating the individual animal care and better attention.

Table 13.3 contains the data on milk yield per animal based on the educational of the milk producers. It was found that collegiate level producers secured first ranks in order of milk yield as it records 6.06 litres, and followed by secondary level, primary level and unlettered respondents and their level of milk yield 5.52, 5.27 and 5.13 respectively. It reveals that the influence of education on milk yield is quite apparent, showing that the higher the educational level of the producers, the higher the milk productivity.

Table 13.3 : Milk Yield per Animal — Education

Education	Illiterate	Primary	Secondary	College	Total Average
Milk Yield (in litres)	5.13	5.27	5.52	6.06	5.38

The data presented in Table 13.4 indicates that occupationwise milk yield per animal per day, it is inferred that those who have practicing the dairy as a main occupation ranks first in order of milk yield as it is calculated as 5.54 litres. Rest of them are doing it as a subsidiary one as it records 5.23 litres of milk yield per animal. It shows that the influence of occupation on milk yield, is significant one. It means main dairy farm experience leads to higher milk productivity. It is evident that gaining more information on feeding mechanism and diagnosis of animal health care by virtue of main occupation results in high quantity of milk output.

Table 13.4 : Milk Yield per Animal — Occupation

Occupation	Main Dairy	Subsidiary Dairy	Total average
Milk Yield (in litres)	5.54	5.23	5.38

Policy Suggestions

In order to increase milk production the milk producers should be persuaded to rear hybrid variety of animals. Further, there is a need to inculcate knowledge about the ways and means of enhancing milk productivity.

Green fodder has a significant positive influence on milk yield. However, majority of the village are unable to provide adequate level of green fodder, due to lack of sufficient grass lands. Therefore, there is a need to provide puramboke lands to the milk producers experimentally for grazing their animals under co-operative basis with a view to cultivate green fodder in collaboration with the Agricultural department. In this connection, necessary arrangement should be made for demonstration plots in each village. The Co-operative Society must invite all the milk producers and train them in the utilization of green fodder.

Majority of the milk producers in South Arcot district low potential village faces the problem of inadequate provision of free veterinary aid and irregular visit of doctors to the villages. The inadequate free veterinary aid is due to lack of sufficient stock of medicines. Therefore, proper stock should be maintained and buffer stock should also be kept. The district authorities should periodically monitor the activities of veterinary doctors in each village. Under the control of milk Co-operative society a veterinary dispensary should be established on the basis of the strength of animal population. To ease the performance of veterinary aid, a self- contained mobile van with medicine and equipments can be introduced to cater to the needs of the milk producer.

Managerial Implications

Human Resource Development

The content and coverage of training should focus on human resource development. This programmer should inculcate skills regarding farm management practice in terms of scientific feeding. This feeding technique includes quantity, timings, quality and adoption of balanced nutritional practice. Another aspect of this training is to impart knowledge about animal health care practice pertaining to artificial insemination and its appropriate time of application, preventive, curative and promotive health care practices, hygienic maintenance of animals and sanitation of the rearing sheds. This will imbibe the awareness about the benefits of rearing hybrid animals. Moreover, to develop cordial relationship between milk producers and officials of the co-operatives, there is a need to impart sensitivity training programme.

Orientation Training

It is drawn from the findings of this study that milk productivity per animal is low among the owners of large herdsize, indicating the inefficiency of farm management practice. Hence, dairy co-operatives should take efforts to improve the operational efficiency by way of conducting a special production oriented training in the respective areas of operation. Concentrate is the major nutrient in increasing milk productivity. The feed and fodder provided by the dairy co-operatives are not up to the expectation in terms of quality and quantity. There is a need to select and procure the best quality or raw materials and mixing the raw materials in the right proportion and this task should be assigned to skilled workers. In addition to that, machines should be properly maintained and renovated.

Quality Circle

Dairy Co-operative should make efforts to develop a quality control circle among milk producers. In this circle, producers should be empowered to chalk out the production aspect relating to quality improvement, enhancing productivity and ways, means of establishing smooth relationship between producers and the co-operative personnel. Further, this circle should have the privilege to advise the district unions and State Federation.

With a view to increase milk supply and productivity, the co-operatives should introduce cash incentive scheme. Producers who supply the best quality as well as more quantity should be rewarded. The same should be extended to the village co-operatives based on the procurement level.

Table 13.5 presents the data on annual milk production and per capita availability of milk in India. In 1950-51 the annual milk production was 17 million tonnes but it rose to 70.8 million tonnes by 1996-97. Thereafter, it is expected to increase further to 86 million tonnes by 2000-2001.

The per capita availability of milk was 132 grams per day in 1950-51 and it went up to 188 grams per day in 1993-94 again it rose to 208 grams per day in 1996-97. It is expected to increase to 233 grams per day by 2000-2001.

The annual growth rate of milk production has been quite

discouraging between 1950 and 1973 and thereafter it has increased progressively due to implementation of Operation Flood in 1970.

Table 13.5 : Annual Milk Production and Per Capita Availability

Financial Year	Production (million tonnes)	Per Capita Availability (gms/day)
1950-51	17.0	132
1955-56	19.0	135
1960-61	20.0	127
1968-69	21.2	113
1973-74	23.2	111
1980-81	31.6	128
1984-85	41.5	148
1985-86	44.0	162
1990-91	53.9	178
1991-92	55.7	181
1992-93	57.6	183
1993-94	60.6	188
1994-95	63.5	194
1995-96	66.3	199
1996-97	70.8	208
1997-98	74.3	214
1998-99	78.0	220
1999-2000	81.9	227
2000-2001	86.0	233
	Average Annual Growth Rates	
1950-60	1.64	
1961-73	1.15	
1974-80	4.51	
1981-90	5.68	
1991-95	4.90	
1996-2000	5.63	

A keen observation of the data in Table 13.6 indicates the regional variation in milk yield in India among different varieties of milk animals. In the northern region, Punjab occupies the first position in milk yield per animal in all varieties of milch animals. In the yield of cross-bred animal, Jammu and Kashmir secures the second position. Rajasthan takes the third position in per animal yield of milk among indigenous species of cows and buffaloes.

In the southern region, Andhra Pradesh occupies the first position in per animal milk yield among cross-bred cows and others lag behind it. Tamil Nadu keeps the first position in per animal milk yield among the indigenous species of cows. In the case of buffaloes milk yield, Pondicherry takes the first position.

Table 13.6 : Milk Yield per Animal 1987-88

(In litres)

Region/States	Cows		Buffaloes
	Indigenous	Crossbred	
NORTHERN			
Haryana	3.143*	—	4.471
Himachal Pradesh	1.177	3.552	3.321
Jammu & Kashmir	1.586	4.987	3.488
Punjab	3.202	6.456	4.778
Rajasthan	2.520	—	3.750
Uttar Pradesh	1.940	—	3.286
SOUTHERN			
Andhra Pradesh	0.975	5.670	2.008
Karnataka	1.418	5.253	2,272
Kerala	1,757	4.523	3.410
Pondicherry	—	—	3.781
Tamil Nadu	2.927	—	3.315
EASTERN			
Andaman & Nicobar	—	—	2.700
Assam	—	—	—
Bihar	1.665	4.945	3.621
Meghalaya	0.570	7.280	2.070
Orissa	0.445	2.442	1.344
Sikkim	—	—	—
West Bengal	2.404	—	5.298
WESTERN			
Gujarat	2.371	7.943	3.361
Madhya Pradesh	1.216	—	3.181
Maharashtra	1.021	5.318	2.719

* Includes Crossbreds.

In the Eastern region, West Bengal occupies the first position in per animal milk yield among the indigenous cows and buffaloes. Meghalaya holds the first position in the case of cross bred yield.

In the Western region, Gujarat occupies the first position in per animal's milk yield among the cross-bred cows.

Impact of Liberalization - GATT

Liberalization policy would affect milk producers in three ways :

(a) by affecting the national economy,
(b) by affecting the business of milk production, and
(c) by affecting the economies of other agricultural commodities since milk producer invariably practices mixed farming system.

Liberalization (GATT) would have both positive as well as negative impact on the economy of milk producers. The delicensing has resulted in higher capital inflow. Consequently, many new dairy plants have been set up in the country. Reduced role of public sector and privatization would result in competition and improved efficiency of the system. It would provide better prices to milk producers. Entry of the multinationals in consumer goods is likely to affect small producers adversely, since multinationals would encourage production by bigger farmers as the hinterland of their processing plant where they can control quality and transportation costs. It is also feared that as a result of GATT there would be a rise in price due to removal of subsidies and increase in the prices of drugs and some feed ingredients.

Future Dairying Scenario

The scenario of Indian dairying has been forecast till the year 2020. The dairying system can be sub-divided into (1) Production and (2) Procurement systems.

Table 13.7 : Present and Future Milch Animal Population

(In million)

Description	Year	
	1996	2020
Indian bovine population		
Cattle	196	228
Buffaloes	80	104
World bovine population		
Cattle	1320	1520
Buffaloes	151	180

It is observed that Table 13.7 shows livestock population of India consisting of 276 million bovine population (of which 196 million comprised cattle and 80 million buffaloes) as in 1996. The bovine population is increasing at the rate of 0.68 per cent for cattle and 0.75 per cent for buffalo per annum. The bovine population is expected to reach 332 million out of which there will be 228 million cattle and 104 million buffalo by the year 2020. Besides there are a host of breeds of cattle number 26 and buffaloes about 7. In India 80 per cent cattle and 60 per cent buffaloes are non-descriptive as well as low producing animals. The world bovine population is growing at the rate of 0.64 per cent for cattle and 0.87 per cent for buffalo. The world bovine population is expected to be 1700 million by the year 2020 out of which there will be 1520 million cattle and 180 million buffaloes.

Table 13.8 : Present and Future Milk Production

(In million tonnes)

Description	Year	
	1996	2020
India's milk production	74.3	220 to 250
World milk production	520.6	620 to 650
India's contribution to world milk production	12 to 15%	30 to 35%

The figures were published in a FAO report in 1997. Table 13.8 gives the milk production as 74.3 million tonnes and it is growing at the rate of five per cent per annum. Therefore, milk production is expected to reach 224.46 million tonnes by the year 2020. The world milk production is about 520.6 million tonnes in the year 1997 and it is expected to increase at the rate of 0.5 per cent to 1 per annum. Thus, by the year 2020, the world milk production is expected to be between 620 and 650 million tonnes per annum. This would mean that India's contribution to world milk production rise from 12 per cent to 30 per cent in the year 2020.

References

Indian Dairy Association, *Dairy India — 1997*, The Author, New Delhi, 1997.

Indian Journal of Dairy Science, Vol. 8, No. 8, 1995, Kang, G.S., Procurement and Milk Marketing in Bihar", *Indian Dairyman,* Vol. 41, No. 6, 1989.

Madan Mohan, C., *Dairy Management in India*, Mittal Publications Delhi, 1989.

Mudgal, V.D., Milk Productivity in various climatic zones of the country, *Indian Dairyman,* August 1995.

Patel, S.M., and Pandey, M.K., "Economic Impact of Kaira District Co-operative Milk Producers Union (AMUL Dairy) in Rural Areas of Kaira district", Ahmedabad, Institute of Co-operative Management, 1976.

Prathap Reddy, "Measuring performance of co-operatives", *Indian Dairyman,* Vol. 45, No.11, 1993.

Rao, C.K., and Rao, C.V., *Textbook of Dairy Science*, S. Bhattacharya & Co., Calcutta, 1966.

Shah, Deepak, Jain, D.K., and Sharma, K.N.S., *Milk Production Functions of Bulandshahr district of Uttar Pradesh.*

The Marketing Research Corporation of India," The Marketing Research Corporation of India Ltd., New Delhi, 1973.

14

PROBLEMS AND POLICY IMPLICATIONS OF SUGAR INDUSTRY : A Perspective Focus on Tamil Nadu

— *R. M. Nagarajan*

India is the world's largest consumer and the second largest producer of sugar, topped only by Brazil. Although, according to industry circles, India produces the cheapest sugar in the world, it is outpriced in the international market because of the interference by the Government and the States. Tamil Nadu is one of the top ranking sugarcane producing States and sugarcane is its major commercial crop. Nearly 2.8 lakh farmers have been cultivating sugarcane in the vast area of 4.4 lakh acres and over 11 crore people are directly or indirectly dependent on the sugar industry in the country.

The objectives of the Sugar Industry are :

* To procure sugarcane from farmers at remunerative price.
* To supply pesticides, fertilizers and crop loan at reasonable cost.
* To arrange proper transport facilities for transporting sugarcane from the farmers field to sugar mill.
* To provide sugarcane payment at earliest.
* To consider levy quota for supplying sugar through public distribution system.

Crisis of Sugarcane Cultivators in Tamil Nadu

The announcement of Rs.1000 per tonne as the SAP for sugarcane with 10 per cent recovery would help only a small section of farmers attached to a few sugar mills. In major parts of the State, the recovery content of sugarcane ranged between 8.5 to 9 per cent as crops were languishing due to want of water consequent to the erratic power supply. In the State only four sugar factories had recorded 10 per cent recovery rate, and as such, the hike would not mean anything to a majority of farmers.

Even now many sugar mills in the State were paying Rs. 900 to 950 per tonne for 10.5 per cent recovery. The main demand of sugarcane farmers was Rs. 1000 per tonne for 8.5 per cent recovery as assured by the DMK during the 1996 election. Hence, a large number of sugarcane growers would not be entitled to the new SAP. It has called upon the Government to remove the conditionality of recovery rate and make available the Rs. 1000 SAP (State Advised Price) uniformly to all sugarcane farmers. During the harvesting period farmers have to pay bribe to the lorry transporters for transporting of sugarcane each and every time. Illegally this is in practice all over Tamil Nadu.

Even then, in many instances, the private mills have failed to honour their commitments. In 1998, the private sugar mills had moved the Madras High Court and obtained an interim order to the effect that the "State Government does not enjoy the rights to fix the SAP, and even if it does so, the private mills would not be bound by the decision." Therefore, in the past two years, the sugar mills have been fixing the cane price at a lower level as dictated by their whims and fancies. Most of the cooperative sugar mills have not paid sugarcane dues yet and also farmers lack ability and capacity to cultivate sugarcane in the next season.

SMP and SAP

As per the sugarcane control order issued under the Essential Commodities Act, the Central Government fixes the Statutory Minimum Price (SMP) for sugarcane below which no sugar factory can pay. However, in practice, the farmers are being paid State Advised Price (SAP) of sugarcane which are substantially higher than SMP. And one of the problems the sugarcane producers face is the presence of a dual authority for sugarcane pricing.

The SMP is fixed by the Government of India, Ministry of Consumer Affairs and Public Distribution (Department of Sugar and Edible Oils). This price has been fixed for the basic sugar recovery of 8.5 per cent with the consultation of the authorities, bodies and associations and also as per the clause 3 of Sugarcane (Control) Order, 1966. The price for the current season has been fixed based on the peak period recovery of previous crushing season. The basic price for 8.5 per cent recovery in 1999-2000 season is Rs. 56.10 per Qtl.

State Advised Price (SAP)

The State Advised Price is the price recommended by the State government. This price is fixed for the basic recovery of 8.5 per cent and also calculated for the peak period recovery of the earlier season. Sugarcane price has been fixed by the State Government by considering the demand of the cane growers' associations and paying capacity of the sugar mills functioning in the State. State Advised Price (SMP) for 1999-2000 was Rs. 90.54 per Qtl.

Most of the sugar mills not only in Tamil Nadu but throughout our country are facing huge loss due to the vulnerable government policies and poor performance of the marketing conditions. At present the sugar mills are paying the cane price according to financial condition of the sugar mills.

In 1998-99, Maharashtra produced 472 lakh tonnes of sugarcane and 53.37 lakh tonnes of sugar in 119 factories; the average recovery was 11.16 per cent. Tamil Nadu produced 467 lakh tonnes of sugarcane; but only 17.30 lakh tonnes of sugar in 36 factories with a recovery of 8.83 per cent. It understood that so much of difference between Maharashtra and Tamil Nadu in the sugarcane recovery rate, namely 11.16 and 8.83 per cent respectively.

Maharashtra has special strengths in sugar production; its strong cooperatives ensure fuller utilisation of cane by the organised sector. In contrast, cooperative sugar mills in Tamil Nadu are weak and have been consistently in the red. A sizable portion of cane produced goes for jaggery production, which is much less efficient in recovery.

The Centre proposes to establish a National Sugarcane Price Fixing Board (NSPFB) for fixing cane prices payable by factories, as against the existing practice wherein prices are determined by individual State governments by way of State Advised Prices (SAP).

Currently, the Centre only fixes the statutory minimum price (SMP) for sugarcane during each season. The SMP, however, merely forms the basis for determination of the price of levy sugar supplies by factories for the public distribution system. The actual cane price paid by mills is the SAP, which is invariably higher than the SMP. During the 1999-2000 season (October-September) for instance, the Centre fixed an SMP of Rs. 56.10 per quintal linked to a basic sugar of 8.5 per cent. But the SAP varied from State to State, with some such as Haryana fixing a much higher cane price of Rs. 104-110 per quintal. This, in turn, has led to mounting cane arrears, with factories claiming that they are not in a position to pay such high "Politically motivated" prices.

During 1998-99, the factories in Maharashtra paid an average cane price of just Rs. 77.42 per quintal, as against Rs. 91-95 fixed by the Punjab and Haryana Government.

Further, the board would not do away with the role of the Commission for Agricultural Costs and Prices (CACP) which will continue to recommend the SMP of cane for each season to determine levy sugar prices. "The board's price will be higher than the SMP, but lower than the SAP that would otherwise be declared by the states."

The cane growers as well as the sugar industry too are in a sad plight. The jump in cane output to 309.30 million tonnes from 295.70 million tonnes in the 1998-99 crushing season has been responsible for the sharp rise in sugar production to 182 lakh tonnes from 155.41 lakh tonnes in 1998-99. As these stocks pose a problem of storage and impose a heavy crippling burden of interest charges, it has been decided to permit exports of 10 lakh tonnes and the sugar mills involved will not be liable to observe levy obligations.

Distribution System

The supply of sugar into the market is controlled by the Central Government. The government has fixed the ratio between levy and free sale sugar as 30.70. The price fixed by the Central Government besides it control the release of sugar under the free sale quota.

From the early '80s till now the government has imposed partial price control. The essence of this policy is that a certain percentage of each sugar mill's production has to be sold as levy sugar at a fixed price for sale through the ration shops.

In the early '80s the burden of levy sugar was as high as 65 per cent, which were reduced in the '90s to 40 per cent and for the current year the levy has been reduced to 30 per cent.

Sugar factories have to sell 30 per cent of the produced sugar to the government for levy price which is fined by the Government of India by incurring 20 per cent loss. Another 70 per cent of the sugar are sold through open market. The dual price policy of sugar affects the efficacy of the sugar factories. The price payable for levy sugar is fixed by Central Government based on the recommendations of the Bureau of Industrial Cost and Prices (BICP).

The current price for levy sugar is about Rs.11 per kg and FPS between Rs. 13.50 to Rs. 13.75 per kg. "These prices are not good enough and most mills are financially bleeding".

During the year 1999, the total sugar production in India was 170 lakh tonnes, out of this 51 lakh tonnes of sugar was allotted as levy quota. Due to this conditionality levy policy of the Government, sugar mills have a financial burden of Rs. 1200 crores every year and also sugar mills have been supplying sugar to Government less than its production cost of 20 per cent.

Sugar Policy in India

At present we have surplus sugar stocks, eventhough our country imports sugar from other countries. Sugar supply and demand ratio in the year 1997-98 is at 149:100. It is understood that the sugar supply is more than the demand. In this situation 19 lakh tonnes of sugar was imported to India in 1997-98. Though we are one of the largest sugar producers in the world, we are not able to export our surplus sugar production. Till march 1998, 8.58 lakh tonnes of sugar had been imported of which about 5.79 lakh tonnes were imported from Pakistan. Between April and July the same year about one lakh tonnes of sugar was imported mostly from Brazil, China and Thailand. Imported sugar is cheaper and the Indian traders earn profit by selling it in the domestic market. This may be economically viable but socially unjustified.

Table 14.1 : World Sugar Production

Sl. No.	Name of the Country	No. of sugar mills	Daily crusing of sugarcane (Tonnes)	Daily production of sugar (Tonnes)
1.	Hawaii	9	4111	44111
2.	Colombia	10	4590	214900
3.	South Africa	13	6877	137769
4.	Mauritius	16	3195	42970
5.	Australia	28	9216	183321
6.	Thailand	45	10307	140540
7.	Mexico	67	4749	71015
8.	Cuba	156	4229	45538
9.	Brazil	213	9168	64018
10.	India	416	2500	33700

Source : Indian Sugar Producers Association (ISPA).

Colombia is the largest sugar producing country in the world and its daily sugar production is 2,14,900 tonnes. The total number of sugar mills in India is 416, but at the same time the crushing capacity and production result of the Indian sugar mills is lower than the other countries. In the world, there are four countries only producing more than 1 lakh tonnes of sugar per day, such as Colombia, Australia, Thailand and South Africa.

Table 14.2 : State-wise Sugar production and consumption in India

Sl. No	Year	Name of the State	Production ('000 tonnes)	Consumption ('000 tonnes)
1.	1998-99	Andhra Pradesh	1,113	830
2.		Assam	4	277
3.		Bihar	258	731
4.		Delhi	—	305
5.		Gujarat	1025	1089
6.		Haryana	403	498
7.		Karnataka	1362	686
8.		Kerala	9	571
9.		Madhya Pradesh	82	851
10.		Maharashtra	5,344	2320
11.		Orissa	73	257
12.		Punjab	312	773
13.		Rajasthan	23	657
14.		Tamil Nadu	1705	1050
15.		Uttar Pradesh	3729	2068
16.		West Bengal	5	899
17.		Other States	53	338
Total		All-India	15,500	14,200

The statistics of the production and consumption of sugar proves that India had enough stock of sugar during the year 1998-99. A comparative analysis of the rate of production and consumption of sugar in Tamil Nadu indicates that production is greater than consumption. In India, Maharashtra has a balanced and prominent production cycle of sugar. Thus, these two States play a decisive role in the economy of the country.

In contrast to these two States, Assam and West Bengal lag far behind in the production of sugar.

Crushing capacity of the Indian sugar mills is lower than the sugar mills of the developed countries. Maximum crushing capacity of the sugar mills in India is 2500 tonnes per day. Whereas in Cuba, Brazil and Australia it is 10,000 tonnes per day. Large scale sugar factories are the felt need of the hour to minimise the cost of production.

Even now many cooperative sugar mills are incurring heavy

loss. During the year 1997-98, the cooperative sugar factories have lost Rs. 360 crores in the State and many of the cooperative sugar mills are not able to run in an effective manner. The cumulative loss of cooperative sugar mills in the State till March this year has touched Rs. 660 crores and it is likely to go up at the end of the current financial year. The State government has come to the rescue of cooperative/public sector mills to overcome the financial crisis by extending financial assistance to the tune of Rs. 158.91 crores to clear the cane price dues to farmers. This year the cooperative sugar mills have sought Rs. 200 crores to clear the arrears.

In most of the Indian Sugar Industry, because of poor payment of salary the employees lack job-satisfaction and interest in the work.

The following are the suggestions to improve the present status of sugar industry and the welfare of the sugarcane growers :

* State government to take immediate steps for the payment of Rs. 600 crores, due as arrears, from the 19 cooperative and public sector sugar mills and 17 private sugar mills. It must be cleared without any further delay.
* The payment of sugarcane should be done within 14 days from the date of sugarcane supplying, as per the Sugarcane Control Order, 1966.
* To avoid bribery to the lorry transporters by the farmers at the time of cane harvesting.
* To make proper transport facilities to bring sugarcane from the field to the mill promptly.
* To increase crushing capacity of the Indian Sugar Industry and to minimise the cost of production.
* To export minimum of 10 lakh tonnes per annum.
* To restrict sugar import from other countries and to collect 50 per cent import duty.
* To reduce levy quota step by step in future.
* To find alternatives to dispose of surplus sugar stocks.
* To avoid technological obsolescence in sugar industry and to make sustainable development through technological upgradation.

Present Status of Sugar Mills in Tamil Nadu

Sugar Industry is one of the major Industries in India. It ranks second among the agro based industries and plays an important role in the economic life of the country. Sugar Industry creates employment to 40 million people and fifty-eight per cent of the total sugar production is contributed by the cooperative sugar mills. In our country three per cent of the total cultivable land is occupied by the sugarcane growers. There are 416 sugar mills functioning in India, of which 116 are in Maharashtra.

India is one of the largest sugar producing countries of the world. Out of 100 million tonnes of sugar produced during the year 1991-92 in the world. India's contribution was 8.5 million tonnes.

Tamil Nadu is one of the top ranking sugar producing States in the country which has suitable agro-climatic condition. There are 36 sugar factories in Tamil Nadu. Of these 17 are run by private entrepreneurs, 16 are under cooperatives and 3 factories are run by the public sector. Due to the buffer stock and irregularity in working of sugar mills in Tamil Nadu more or less all the sugar factories are running in heavy loss and most of the sugar mills cannot pay even cane arrears to farmers timely. Due to this financial burden, viability and efficiency of the sugar mills are affected. Now all the cooperative sugar mills are running in heavy loss and incurring huge financial burden.

During the year 1998-99, the financial demand of the sugar mills from the Government of Tamil Nadu was Rs. 450 crores for the effective running and survival of the sugar factories. Therefore, the situation of sugar factories and sugarcane cultivators in Tamil Nadu are considerably very worst.

From the table out of the 17.935 thousand tonnes were produced in India during 1996-97, 8655 thousand tonnes were from the cooperative sector, out of the 416 factories in operation 232 from the cooperative sector.

Table 14.4 shows sugar production in Tamil Nadu

Table 14.3 : Scenario of Indian Sugar Industry

Year	Area under cane '000 hectares	Yield under cane '000 hectares	Production of cane '000 tonnes	No. of Factories in operation	Total Sugar produced in '000 tonnes
1930-31	1,176	30.9	36,354	28	120
1940-41	1,617	32.1	51,978	148	1,113
1950-51	1,707	40.5	69,220	138	1,103
1955-56	1,846	39.3	72,692	143	1,862
1960-61	2,456	45.0	1,10,554	173	3,028
1965-66	2,836	43.7	1,23,990	200	3,532
1970-71	2,615	48.3	1,26,368	216	3,740
1975-76	2,762	50.9	1,40,604	253	4,261
1980-81	2,667	57.8	1,54,248	314	5,147
1985-86	2,862	60.0	1,71,681	341	7,016
1990-91	3,680	65.4	2,41,046	385	12,046
1994-95	3,815	71.1	2,71,229	408	14,643
1996-97	—	—	2,84,000	416	17,935

Source : The Cooperator.

Table 14.4 : Sugar Production in Tamil Nadu

Sl. No.	Year	Sugar Production (In lakh tonnes)
1.	1991-92	1,327
2.	1992-93	1,021
3.	1993-94	1,122
4.	1994-95	1,921
5.	1995-96	1,671
6.	1996-97	1,050

Source : The Cooperator, Vol. XXX, No.10, April 1998.

From the above table sugar production in Tamil Nadu was increased to 1,327 lakh tonnes during 1991-92. But at the same time the sugar production was decreased to 1050 lakh tonnes in 1996-97.

The average sugar price in Tamil Nadu is depicted in Table 14.5.

Table 14.5 : Average Sugar Price in Tamil Nadu

Sl. No	Year	Levy (Rs. in '000)	Free Market (Rs. in '000)
1.	1991-92	602.71	844.25
2.	1992-93	719.78	1003.42
3.	1993-94	764.23	1278.42
4.	1994-95	782.46	1133.83
5.	1995-96	937.38	1261.33
6.	1996-97	1049.04	1245.76
7.	1997-98	1140.00	1380.00

Source : The Cooperator, Vol. XXX XI, No. 10, April 1998.

Export of Sugar

The real thrust in India's export of sugar in 1991-92 with record export of 17.88 lakh tonnes valued at Rs. 524.42 crores (Table 14.6). Thereafter the same tempo could not be maintained due to the wide fluctuations in sugar production and rapid increase in domestic consumption.

Table 14.6 : Export of Sugar from 1990-91 to 1996-97

Sl. No.	Year	Export Quantity	Export Value (Rs. in crores)
1.	1990-91	12.24	412.34
2.	1991-92	17.88	524.42
3.	1992-93	17.41	514.51
4.	1993-94	10.88	318.64
5.	1994-95	14.71	478.31
6.	1995-96	14.87	481.11
7.	1996-97	13.12	443.18

Source : Secondary data.

The cooperative sector occupies an important place in the Indian sugar industry. An effective starting point for the sugar industry in the cooperative sector was provided by the establishment of cooperative sugar mills at Pravaranagar in Maharashtra. The success of this cooperative sugar mill inspired the growers and State authorities elsewhere to promote similar organisation.

References

Gurumoorthy, T. R., "Sugar Import Socially Unjustified", *Kisan World,* November 1999, Vol. 26, No.11.

Mookerji, Nikil, "Sugar glut: Blame it on the Government's sloppy policy" *Indian Express,* August 28, 2000.

Nagarajan, R. M., "Performance of the sugar cooperative in the functional areas of the management — A case study", M. Coop Project submitted to Gandhigram Rural Institute, Gandhigram, April 1999.

"SAP intended to benefit only private sugar mills" , *The Hindu,* July 23, 2000.

Seshan, P. A., "Paradoxes in economy's growth phase", *The Hindu,* August 31, 2000, p.27.

"Sugarcane ryots plan stir demanding payment of arrears", *The Hindu,* July 5, 2000, p.5.

"Sugar mills debt burden will increase", *The Hindu,* July, 21, 2000.

Thagaval Surangam, *Thinamalar,* January 31, 2000.

15

BEEDI INDUSTRY IN RURAL AREAS : An Overview

— *P. Anandha Rajakumar*

The beedi industry occupies a prominent place in rural development in terms of its capacity to offer potential employment opportunities to a large number of people. It employs over three million workers mostly consisting of adult females and children. In addition, another 40 lakhs are estimated to be seasonally engaged in tendu leaf collection. While 90 per cent of the work force in beedi industry comprise of women and female children, the tendu collection is done predominantly by the tribals. The beedi industry is a major informal sector in Andhra Pradesh, Maharashtra, Tamil Nadu, Uttar Pradesh and West Bangal. In Tamil Nadu State, places such as Tiruchirapalli, Tirunelveli and Vellore are the major centres of beedi production.

Beedi industries earned a foreign exchange of Rs. 806 crores annually and had a turnover of Rs. 19,000 crores every year which contributed substantially to the national economy. In spite of advantages attached with the beedi sector, it has its own limitations, especially in the system of production. The prevailing relations of production subject the workers to ruthless exploitation in many ways. Apart from these, the macro economic environment in Indian context as well as operation of mini cigarette companies jeopardise the beedi in general. Therefore, this chapter takes a comprehensive look at the following aspects :

1. relations of production in the beedi sector,
2. exploitative conditions of workers, and
3. operation of economic policies and its implications for the beedi sector.

Table 15.1 : Concentration of Beedi Workers in Tamil Nadu

District	No. of Workers
Tirunelveli and Tuticorin	5,50,000
Vellore	1,50,000
Tiruchirapalli	15,000
Chennai	15,000
Chengalpattu	10,000
Salem	5,000
Erode	2,000
	7,47,000

Source : A status report of UNICEF, Madras, 1995.

Table 15.1 shows the concentration of beedi workers in Tamil Nadu State which include child labour. In all these districts, workers are invariably women and female children. In most of the places beedi rolling is done at home. Involvement of middlemen is so popular. According to available data, it is learnt that beedi rolling is a predominant activity being pursued especially in Tirunelveli and Vellore districts on account of agricultural backwardness.

System of Production

In the beedi industry the following systems of production can be identified.

1. Factory System, and
2. Home-based System.

In the factory system, the process of beedi making takes place at the factory site itself under the direct supervision of the staff members appointed for this purpose like any other industrial organisations. The wage payment is made piece-wise and each worker is required to turn out a fixed minimum quantity of beedis in proportion to raw materials supplied.

In the home based system, the home of the workers is the production site. In this system the distribution of raw materials, collection of beedis and disbursal of wages is made by the management, either through a person, who is employed by the company or through a commission agent, who is not a regular employee of the company but is paid a commission on the basis of production performance under his control. The large sized companies have generally preferred to operate through the commission agents, for this system entails lesser accountability and risk, and contrarily greater manoeuvrability and profit.

Production Relations in Operation

There are two important points from where raw materials are supplied to the beedi workers. The companies located in cities/ towns supplies raw materials in bulk to its own branches and middlemen in the villages, to supply back finished beedis which is proportionate to the amount of raw materials supplied to them. The branches directly run by companies are called as company shops and shops run by middlemen/agents are known as commission shops. Both the shops are involved in distribution of raw materials in fixed quantities to the workers who take them to their houses for rolling beedis.

Both the company and commission shops are run parallel by owners and middlemen respectively who have specific geographical territory for operation. At any given time, a company will have number of middlemen besides its own branches run through persons appointed by company owners. A beedi shop shall cover one village or a cluster of villages depending upon the need, capacity to operate and production potential in terms of availability of workers. It is possible that in a village there may be more than one commission shop and company shop as well. Contrastingly one worker rolling beedis simultaneously for different middlemen does not arise due to the fact that these contractors are identified themselves as competitors in the field of beedi production. In general, large villages will have huge number of beedi rollers with many number of middlemen and also agents of company run branches.

It is obvious that factory owner is the principal employer who operates through their own branches directly and indirectly through middlemen. Thus, middlemen are encouraged by company owners to take up the task of production. This is the typical pattern of production relations identified in the beedi sector.

Family *Vs.* Industrialists

Production of beedis takes place within the household, rather than through formal market organisations. Family as an important social institution is responsible for establishment and maintenance of household in any society. Therefore, there is a clear cut interface between the institution of family and production organisation both directly and indirectly in the beedi sector. This interface is to be studied in terms of role played by middlemen which is unique in beedi production.

In the system of beedi production family as an institution can be treated at one extreme while the industrialists from the other part. But an interesting situation is that the institution of family and industrialists are brought in relations of production by middlemen.

The value of a product is the amount of human labour which goes into the making of it. The industrialists make profit through middlemen while exchanging the product on the market. This margin of difference (the profit) between the price the owner of means of production received for the product on the market, and the price he paid to the workers for their labour (wages) is therefore appropriated.

It is understood from the system of production in the beedi

sector that, on the basis of material product and means of production, families in a given area come to have determinate relations to means of production and thus they have determinate class relations. It is in this class pattern, industrialists as a class possess the means of material production at their disposal, has control over the other class (workers) in the existing framework of production relations. This control is being exercised through middlemen supported system of production.

This production arrangement which favours the industrialists is effectively strengthened by the involvement of middlemen. Therefore, the predominant role played by middlemen cannot be overlooked. Middlemen are the instruments in facilitating beedi production and they are the real beneficiaries next to the owners of beedi companies. And thus, existing production relations is not beneficial in everyway to the beedi workers.

Division of Labour in the Beedi Sector

The relations of production do not confine to human producers and nature, it very much exists between the human beings themselves due to their different locations in the society as a result of the division of labour which is a fundamental feature of human population. An important feature indentified with beedi rolling profession is predominant engagement of females. It is learnt from the Indian context that beedi rolling is 'feminised'. Thus, females as a separate category of workers are brought in production relations by middlemen since the work is carried out at the household level. This home-based production is solely responsible for perpetuation of exploitation and exclusive induction of females.

Property Relations in the Beedi Sector

In beedi production, company owners are possessing all means of production. But for their convenience they engage middlemen who acts as kingpin in the process of production. Another important aspect in property relations is that middlemen themselves are holding huge amount of wealth and properties in a given locality. It can be noted in several places that middlemen are entrusted with the responsibility of getting beedi production done by the owners of companies only in the pretext of properties possessed by the middlemen and also their location in the social structure of a society. Therefore, it is understood from the property relations in beedi production that propertied classes comprised of both company owners and the middlemen are unitedly involved in production of beedis.

Comparison between Company and Commission System of Production

Following table shows the comparison between company shops and commission shops involved in beedi production. This comparative perspective would help us to understand the extent of exploitation perpetuated towards women by the middlemen in the process of production.

	Company System	Commission System
1.	Flexible in approach relating to production of beedis.	Rigid in approach.
2.	Supply of passbook is done promptly leading to proper flow of benefits like bonus and other claims of workers.	Supply of chitta is popular so that middlemen can escape from liabilities
3.	Frequency of rejecting beedis due to defectiveness is less.	Rejection is common and frequent with cruelty.
4.	Supply of quality raw materials is possible.	Poor quality raw materials are supplied leading to financial burden.
5.	Shops are run with proper licence.	Shops are run illegally at night times without licence.
6.	Workers are informed about various benefits meant for them.	Workers are not properly informed of the benefits.
7.	Exploitation is minimal	Exploitation is severe.

Note : Comparison is made between these two systems of production, based on the authors' field experience in Tirunelveli district of Tamil Nadu.

Sources of Exploitation

In the home based production system, there is a large-scale violation of the legal framework leading to ruthless exploitation. A huge number of workers neither given appointment letter nor a passbook that would fetch them welfare benefits under the legal provisions. Therefore, the conditions of the workers are insecure and they are at the mercy of the middlemen.

An important form of harassment that the workers complain is regarding the underweighing of raw materials (tobacco dust and leaves). The raw materials supplied to them is of poor quality. Therefore, the deficit has to be met by the worker by obtaining materials from the open market or from the middlemen one who run beedishops. Under this circumstance, the workers are expected to supply extra beedis (commission beedis) for every 1000 beedis rolled. But the amount of raw materials supplied to the workers is not even sufficient for producing 1000 beedis. This is the commission given to middlemen in the form of beedis. Therefore, the workers are doubly burdened.

Yet another cruel practice is the merciless rejection of beedis at the time of collection by the middlemen on the ground of quality checking. For the beedis rejected, the workers not only lose wages but also required to compensate the loss. This leads to wage cut severely. It is used as a principal weapon by the middlemen to exercise control over the workers. Above all, the workers are sexually harassed and exploited in the beedi sector.

Reasons for Proliferation of Home-based Beedi Production

The reasons for the shift to home based system are not very difficult to find. Such reasons are listed below :

1. The factory system meant the regularisation of the conditions of work and payment of minimum wages and benefits as per the laws, the avoidance of which would be difficult in the factory system.

2. The factory system involves a substantial expenditure on the space, especially in the urban centres.
3. Since the factory site, where the workers used to gather and work together, hold the possibility of interaction and solidarity leading to collective action.

The beedi company owners learning from the experiences consciously avoided factory based production and there is a shift in the production system in which the workers are removed from each other *vis-a-vis* from the company owners. The beedi company owners, thus, increasingly inclined to prefer the home based manufacturing. Through this it is not only possible to reduce the production cost by cutting expenditure on factory site and maintenance, and by paying lower wages to the workers but also keep them disorganised so that the possibility of unity among them is prevented. Above all, the female workers find it convenient to work at home as it facilitate them to attend to their household activities even while rolling beedis (Srinivasulu, 1997).

Prevailing Economic Policies and Beedi Sector

In 1991 Union Budget, excise reduction from Rs. 120 to Rs. 60 was announced for cigarettes less than 60 mm length. The cigarettes available in the market can be broadly classified into filtered and non-filtered. The excise duty varies according to the size of the cigarette in both the types. With the reduction of excise duty, most of the cigarette companies (ITC, GTC, UST, Goodfrey Phillips) started production of 59 mm length non-filter cigarettes which have come to be identified as mini cigarettes.

The price difference between mini cigarettes and beedis becoming negligible, and the mini cigarettes poses threat to the beedi sector. And thus, accelerated production of mini cigarettes have led to the reduction of work in the beedi sector. What is critical at this juncture that threat of mini cigarettes has been used as a pretext by the company owners/middlemen to force the workers to accept the wages offered by them and also deprive them of certain privileges as per legal provisions. This is an evidence available at hand to show policy of the Government which poses serious threat to the very existence of cottage industries in the villages.

References

Basas Eswara, K.V. & Prasad, H., *"Beedi Workers in Central India: A study on living conditions"*, Ministry of Labour, Govt. of India, 1988.

Eswara, K.V & Anuradha (1986), "State and unorganised labour - A study of Home workers in Beedi Industry in central India" in Patel. B.R (Ed.) *Problems of Home Based Workers in India,* (Proceedings of a National Workshop held at Ahmedabad, Oxford & IBH Publishing Co. Pvt. Ltd., New Delhi.

Karunanithi, G., "Child labour in North Arcot, Ambedkar District — An Indepth study of pledged children in Beedi works", Project report submitted to ICSSR, New Delhi, 1995.

Karunanithi, G. "Plight of pledged children in Beedi works", *Economic and Political Weekly,* February 28, 1999.

Mohamer, Asfak Hosain, "Exploitation of women and child labour in Beedi industry in Samsarganj, *Child Workers in Asia",* October-December 1989, Vol. 3(4), (reproduced from *Social Welfare,* April 1987).

Pande, Rekha, "Child labour in Beedi Industry in Nizamabad District of Andhra Pradesh", Ministry of Labour, Govt. of India, 1980.

16

PROBLEMS OF HANDLOOM SECTOR

— *T. R. Gurumoorthy* and *N. R. Rengachari*

Introduction

Handloom is an important traditional craft of India. Handloom being a traditional, rural and semi-urban cottage industry is highly labour intensive in character. It is spread over several parts of the country and covers not only the clothing needs of the people but also provides substantial surplus for export for earning foreign exchange of the nation. Thus, the handloom industry occupies an important place in the decentralized sector of the Indian economy. In terms of employment, the handloom industry is next in importance to agriculture. Handloom accounts for over 20 per cent of the cloth produced in the country.

The production of handloom cloth is concentrated in three States viz., Tamil Nadu, Andhra Pradesh and Uttar Pradesh. Of these three States Tamil Nadu has the highest concentration of handloom and handloom weavers in the country. It is estimated that nearly 10 million people all over the country are employed in handloom sector of which Tamil Nadu accounts for over one million people employed in this cottage industry. Realising the importance of handloom sector the Central Government as well as State Governments have separate ministries to take care of the welfare of handloom weavers and development of handloom industry.

Role of Co-operatives in Handloom Sector

The handloom weavers have always suffered from acute poverty, poor credit worthiness, inability to obtain raw materials and lack of market for their products. To provide financial aid and technical assistance and to strengthen the bargaining power of weavers, it is necessary that they should be brought within an organization. It has been realized that no organization other than co-operatives can suit them better. Therefore efforts were directed towards bringing weavers into the co-operative fold. Co-operative is an economic institution promoted by the people with the patronage of the government for the betterment of the common economic interest. The Tamil Nadu government realized as early as in 1905 the need to organise a co-operative movement in the handloom sector. A Weavers Co-operative Society at Kancheepuram was formed in the year 1905. Later more co-operative societies have been established. At present in Tamil Nadu alone more than 1400 primary handloom co-operatives are functioning catering to the needs of over 3 lakh 60 thousand weaver members.

Statement of the Problem

There are more than ten million people on handloom sector in India. It is the main occupation for their livelihood. Handlooms supply more than 20 per cent of the total cloth manufactured in our country. To protect the weavers as well as the craft the government has come forward to start co-operatives and bring handloom weavers into the ambit of co-operative sector. The increase in the number of handloom co-operatives to 1400 as on date is not sufficient to tap all handloom weavers. Majority of handloom weavers are toiling for their bread lying within the clutches of private sector under master weavers. They are not paid adequate and reasonable wages. As a result they become poorest of the poor. If this situation is unchecked many people will have to give up weaving and hunt for other employment. Therefore it is the felt need of the hour to take care of the social welfare of weaving community and make them lead a decent living by solving the various problems affecting the growth and development of this sector, hence this study.

Objectives of the Study

The specific objectives of this study are listed as follows :

(i) To study the problem of input shortage in handloom sector;
(ii) To analyse the problem of accumulation of huge stock in handloom industry;
(iii) To study the problem of poor working capital in handloom sector;
(iv) To study the problem of marketing strategy in vogue in the handloom sector;
(v) To analyse the problem of instability in pricing of handloom goods;
(vi) To study the problem of inefficient management of handloom industry;
(vii) To give suggestions for overcoming these problems for the growth and development of handloom sector in India.

Methodology

This study is descriptive and analytical and it is based on secondary data. The required secondary data for the purpose of analysis and interpretation of the study are collected from *Economic Survey,* Government of India; Statistical Handbook of Tamil Nadu. An Economic Appraisal, Evaluation and Applied Research Department, Government of Tamil Nadu; Doctoral Theses of eminent professors; M.Phil. Dissertations and relevant books, leading journals, periodicals and newspapers.

The problems retarding the growth and development of handloom sector were identified by researcher through informal interviews with Presidents of Primary Handloom Cooperative Societies, Master Weavers and Weavers. The researcher has also ascertained the problem sector through discussions held with officials of Directorate of Handlooms, Tamil Nadu.

Problems of Handloom Sector — An Analysis

Shortage of Input

The handloom industry is in need of cotton yarn, silk, art silk, dyes and chemicals and zari. Handloom Cooperatives purchase yarn from the co-optex and private traders. Master weavers of big and small and other weavers procure the required raw materials only from private traders. The supply of yarn is not regular. At the same time fluctuations prevails in the price of yarns. The price of yarn is high with private traders comparing the price of cooptex. Hence the availability of different counts of yarn and other raw materials in the right price and in the right time is the serious problem of handloom weavers.

Accumulation of Huge Stock

The handloom industry is suffering from poor sales and the consequent accumulation of huge stock over the years. The production is a continuous function in the handloom sector. But the sales is seasonal. An increase in sales takes place only during festival seasons. During these seasons rebate is allowed by primary handloom societies at specified rates by the Government of Tamil Nadu Co-optex procures only 50 per cent of the production of the handloom societies. Sufficient demand is not available to sell the remaining 50 per cent of production in the textile market.

Poor Working Capital

Poor Working Capital is one of the problems affecting the working of handloom sector. Due to poor working capital the industry is not able to purchase yarn in the open market, when the price declines. The handloom industry is not able to procure large quantity of yarn from the Cooptex and pay wages in time to weavers due to inadequate working capital.

Lack of Marketing Strategy

Marketing strategy has been unknown to the handloom sector. Ascertaining the demand in the market, production based upon demand, application of marketing concept and application of consumer oriented approach are not in practice in the handloom industry. So the industry is not able to withstand competition in the textile market and suffer a lot from poor sales and huge accumulation of stock.

Inadequacy of Pricing

Pricing is one of the major problems of the handlooms sector. The price of handloom fabrics fixed by the society covers only the direct expenses known as cost of raw materials and wages. It does not cover indirect expenses known as overheads. The society fixes certain percentage of profit over the direct expenses. If the overhead lies within the stipulated percentage of profit, the society can get profit, otherwise it will suffer loss. So the pricing policy is not the reasons for the loss sustained by handloom industry.

Inefficient Management

Inefficient management is also one of the problem of the handloom industry. Retail and bulk sales occupy a predominant position in the total sales of handloom sector. The retail and bulk sales depend upon the efficiency of the administration. The management should function with foresight and adapt itself to the needs and requirements of consumers. Without delay necessary improvements should be made in the design and texture of handloom fabrics so that it is able to maintain market share and also withstand competition from mill fabrics.

Suggestions for Better Performance of Handloom Sector

1 The problem of shortage of input can be solved by the government. It has to estimate the total yarn requirements of

the handloom sector and procure the requirements from spinning mills. The government has to take necessary steps to distribute the entire production of spinning mills to the handloom weavers. The capacity of the spinning mills may be increased to solve the problem of yarn requirement of handloom weavers. The National Textile Corporation and South India Mills Association have to enhance their assistance with regard to yarn supply to handloom weavers through co-operatives. Handloom industry purchases dyes and chemicals from private merchants. The governments has to take reasonable steps to supply dyes and chemicals to the handloom industry. For example, the Government of Tamil Nadu has established Vanavil Dyes and Chemical Project at Cuddalore in South Arcot District. This project is directed by the government to supply dyes and chemicals to the handloom sector as and when they require at reasonable prices in Villupuram and Cuddalore areas in Tamil Nadu.

2 To avoid the problem of accumulation of huge stock the Cooptex may be directed by the government to increase the quantity of its procurement. The Cooptex may be directed to promote salesmanship. If it is done, sales will increase in the Cooptex show room, side by side the procurement of Cooptex from the handloom cooperatives and other master weavers will increase. The Cooptex and the handloom cooperatives should jointly promote the publicity of handloom fabrics through fairs and exhibitions at important cities.

The Government of India on 15th, April 1950 passed an order to reserve certain items of fabrics exclusively for the handloom sector. The reserved fabrics are :

(i) Dhoti with borders which contain coloured yarn exceeding 1/4" in width or use Zari or Munga or art silk yarn in dhoti border.

(ii) Lungi Sarang or Gamcha with a check pattern having a

width between 42″ and 52″.

(iii) Chaddars, Bed Sheets, Bed Covers and Counterpanes.

(iv) Low Reed Pick Cloth.

(v) Table Cloth, Napkins, Dusters, Coarse Cloth of Plain Weave, Sarees and Towels.

If the government prohibits the mill sector to produce the above mentioned items with an iron hand it will create good hope to the handloom industry in the textile market. Accumulation of stock will decline and better sales can be promoted.

3 To solve the problem of poor working capital with handloom weavers especially handloom cooperatives, the Cooptex has to settle its due to handloom cooperatives as and when procurement of fabrics is made. If the government settle rebate claim due promptly, considerable part of working capital would not be locked up. The handloom sector should improve their collection policy. The debtors paying promptly may be given cash discount.

4 For better marketing strategy the handloom industry has to apply marketing concept rather than sales concept which has been applied so far. Estimating the demand in the market and production based upon the demand refers to the marketing concept. So the handloom industry has to re-estimate the demand in the market. Based upon the demand they should change their production pattern and design to promote sales. For successful programme of marketing, constant feedback of market intelligence and setting up strong production base are essential.

The handloom industry has to bring many significant changes in the handloom fabrics to suit the taste and preferences of the consumers in recent years. Rational motives like price, quality, quantity, durability and the like and emotional motives like comfort and social status and social factors like age, sex and like play vital role in the marketing of handloom fabrics.

So the handloom industry has to adopt this strategy to fulfil the rational and emotional motives in marketing handloom fabrics.

Market intelligence is preferred in the overseas market. Although the garments of mixed blends have become very popular in overseas market, very little is being done towards the use of synthetic yarn in the weaving of handloom cloth. In view of the prevailing high price of cotton yarn and also the current preference for blended fabrics in export markets it would be advantageous for India to go in for blended fabrics with appropriate mix of different materials according to the requirements of the overseas market.

In the field of export, the Export Promotion Council has to ascertain and predict the demand for handloom industry to produce handloom fabrics based upon the demand in the overseas market to promote export. All India Handloom Board has to increase its substantial marketing support to the handloom industry. The Cooptex has to develop its export wing known as "Cooptex International" to promote the export of handloom fabrics. This export wing to improve the export of handloom fabrics more than what it now does.

The handloom industry has to adopt consumer oriented approach in their production and marketing field rather than the outdated product oriented approach to promote the market of handloom fabrics. At the same time for the survival and growth of handloom industry, the weavers have to possess the outlook of satisfying the consumer needs. They should come forward to take up the programmes of diversification of the existing products, introduction of new products and adoption of suitable product mix in the handloom sector for promoting the market of handloom fabrics. The weavers should be innovative in their work. The handlooms mat be projected to produce polyester shirtings and polyester sarees to catch the home demand as well as overseas demand. During the year 1999-2000 Tamil Nadu State ranked first in exporting handloom goods worth Rs. 25 crore. For the current year it has plans to increase the exports to Rs. 100 crore.

In tune with the fast changing fashions, styles and preferences of the consumers and to meet the increasing demand in the internal and international market for new handloon fabrics, the handloom cooperatives could adopt the modern techniques of weaving. The government has to encourage handloom industry to undertake renovation and modernization of looms. The government has to train weavers to improve the latest designs to suit the latest demand for promoting the market of handloom fabrics. The Government of Tamil Nadu is imparting three months training for manufacture of new varieties in handlooms, by earmarking Rs. 5 lakhs. To enable weavers to produce quality handloom products and to market the same Training Camps are being organized by National Handloom Development Council. Moreover, handloom sector has to change its product mix to remain active in the market. It can also think of producing pyjama, banians, petticoats, underwear for ladies, gents and children according to market requirement. Handloom sector should also enter the market of readymade garments, where there is a vast scope for it. The design- cum-service centres established by the Cooptex have to produce new designs to catch the attention of the customers.

The Handloom Export Promotion Council, All India Handloom Board and Cooptex should act as catalyst agents in the production area and their sales forecast should be translated into a meaningful production and marketing plan to achieve a sound sales base. A chain of district research centre on handlooms, aided and encouraged by the government, can bring about far reaching results in production and marketing of mainstream of dynamic change and make it modern and rigorous.

5 To solve the problem of pricing, the pricing policy of the handloom sector is to be revised. The cost of production includes the cost of raw materials and wages and does not include office administration, selling and distribution expenses and the like. These expenses may be included in the total cost. Collection, allocation and apportionment of

overhead is not in practice in the handloom cooperatives. If it is followed properly, the overhead will be included in the total cost. So the handloom sector may be directed to proceed with the collection, allocation and apportionment of the overhead. Avoiding overheads in the total cost of production reduces the profit of handloom sector and in some circumstances it creates loss to the owners of handlooms.

6. The problem of inefficient management can be solved by setting aside the present procedure of appointing the Board of Directors in the handloom cooperatives by the Assistant Director of Handloom and Textiles. If it is done so, politics will not enter in the appointment of Board of Directors and day-to-day administration of handloom cooperatives. Inefficient persons will not become directors of the societies. Hence the handloom cooperatives will become efficient. So the Board of Directors have to be elected by the weavers of the society in order to run the society in an efficient way.

In the case of big and small master weavers who comprise the rest of the handloom industry apart from cooperatives, they should not be lethargic in taking important decisions. They have to rise to the occasion of stock, inadequate prices for fabrics, outdated designs and technology and the like. They should keep their doors open to welcome modernization of looms, new designs and texture, new marketing concept for handloom fabrics, so that the units are managed efficiently and effectively to yield sizable profit to handloom sector.

References

Arulanandam, M.A., "A Study of the Handloom Industry in Tamil Nadu", Unpublished Research Thesis, Madurai Kamaraj University, 1980.

"Aspects of Handloom Export Marketing", *The Tamil Nadu Journal of Co-operative,* Vol. 70, No. 4 & 5, October, November 1978.

Chidambaram, K., "A Study of the Handloom Pure Silk Industry in Tamil Nadu", Unpublished Research Thesis, Madurai Kamaraj University, 1985.

"Cotton Production Needs to be stepped up", *Financial Express,* September 25, 1993.

Government of India, Economic Survey, 1998-1999 and 1999-2000. *All India Handloom Board Statistical Bulletin.*

Gurumoorthy, T.R., "New Life for a Traditional Industry", *Economic Times*, May 13,1990.

Handloom Export Promotion Council — *Commodity Note on Handlooms*, 1968.

"Handloom Industry in Paramakudi", *Valarthozhil*, August 16-31, 1992.

Handlooms and Textiles Policy and Programmes, Govt. of Tamil Nadu, 1983-84.

"Handlooms in Co-operative Sector", *The Co-operator*, Vol. XXIX, No. 2, July 15, 1991.

Indian Express, dated 28th April, 1984.

Indian Express, dated 2nd September, 1985.

Kamat, G.S. "Revitalizing Handloom - Need for Strong Integrated Structure", *The Tamil Nadu Journal of Co-operation*, Vol. 69, No.1, July 1997.

Kanthiah *et al. A Study of Handloom Sector to increase productivity, reduce costs and improve quality*, 1978.

—— *Survey of Handloom Industry in Madras States* - 1955-56, Bombay, All India Handloom Board, 1959.

—— *Statistical Handbook of Tamil Nadu*, Directorate of Economics and Statistics, 1998.

Mangleek, Girish, "Marketing Strategy for Handloom Co-operatives", *Tamil Nadu Journal of Co-operation*, Vol. 92, No. 5, August 2000.

"Modernisation in Handloom Sector — Felt Need for Survival", *Tamil Nadu Journal of Co-operation*, Vol. 49, December 1992.

"New Life to Handlooms", *Kisan World*, Vol. 20, No. 2, July 1993.

"Social Obligations of Handloom Co-operatives", *The Co-operator*, May, 1992.

Sundar Singh, John, D.K., *The Handloom Industry in Madurai City*, Publications Division, Madurai Kamaraj University, 1981.

Tamil Nadu — An Economic Appraisal, Evaluation an Applied Research Department, Govt. of Tamil Nadu, 1996.

Tamil Nadu — "The Leader in Exporting Handloom Cloth", *Kootturavu*, November 2000.

Thanulingam, N. and Gurumoorthy, T.R., Financial Performance of Handloom Co-operatives — A Study in Paramakudi Town, *Indian Co-operative Review*, Vol. XXV, No. 2, October 1987.

Venkataraman, K.S., *The Handloom Industry in South India*, 1935.

17

INDIAN COTTON HANDLOOM EXPORTS IN A GLOBALISED ECONOMY

— *S. Benjamin Christopher* and *R. Nagarajan*

Introduction

The economic reforms in India emphasises international competitiveness and higher export growth. Discussion of industrial competitiveness in India mostly focus on policies with respect to trade, exchange rate and macro economic stability. The advent of global markets and integrated international production have direct consequences for India's competitiveness. There is evidence that the superior export performance of East Asian firms is partly attributable to their strategic use of cross-national production networks that organise across national borders, production, procurement, distribution, research and development, design, and support services in a given industry.

The primary objective of economic policy reforms has been to accelerate economic growth for which the efficiency of the manufacturing sectors through increased competitive pressure and access to imported inputs at international prices is considered critical. However, India's share of world export markets is very low, at 0.60 per cent in 1996, relative to many other Asian development countries. Also the share of manufactures exports in total exports had remained stagnant at around 74 to 75 per cent in the 1990s. Given the emphasis on export-oriented development, it is especially important to understand the nature of the global production system that shapes the integration of Third World countries like India into the international economy. Achieving a higher level of export grown is critical to Indian Industry's programme of restricting in the globalising economy (Ramasamy, 2000).

In recent years, most countries of Asia have been implementing economic reforms which include policies for macro economic stabilisation as well as structural adjustment. Stabilization policy generally aims to reduce economic imbalances, e.g. budgetary deficit, balance of payment deficit, and inflationary gap. Structural adjustment policies on the other hand are designed to achieve the long-term objectives of making an economy more efficient and competitive by replacing the inward-looking growth strategy with an outward-looking one and by reducing the role of the State in the economy. The latter includes wide-ranging reforms in the areas of regulating framework, ownership of enterprises (e.g. privatization, increased private sector participation etc.), financial sector, taxation and public expenditure, trade and exchange rate measures, technology and so on (Rizwanual, 1996). Some of these measures, especially those aimed at increasing the efficiency and competitiveness of the economy and making it more outward-looking are contributing to the process of globalisation which is going on in the world in general. In this sense, globalisation has to be considered an important aspect of economic reforms that have under way in Asian countries.

The process of economic reforms initiated by the Congress government headed by Mr. Narashima Rao in June 1991 has completed nine years. Although the period is not a very long to assess the impact of economic reforms, it cannot also be considered as too short a period not to merit evaluation. An effort has, therefore, been started to assess the impact of reform measures on the economy (Datt and Sundaram, 2000). As a part of the structural adjustment programme adopted in 1991, efforts have been made to stabilize the economy and deregulate industry, trade and finance so as to increase competition in the country.

Underlying the reforms was the hope founded in neo-classical theory and experience of East Asian Economies that a non-discriminatory trade regime and an economic environment hospitable to Foreign Direct Investment (EDI) would raise the growth rate to sustainable high levels where exports would pay for imports and make the country truly self-reliant (Desphpande and Deshpande, 1996).

Handloom Industry in India

The Indian textile industry has a vital role to play in the nation's economy. This is the single largest in the country as it accounts for 20 to 25 per cent in the total industrial production index. It employs about 20 million people and earns as much as 27 per cent of the country's total export earnings. It is the base on which the pyramid of the industrial sector of the country has been built. What started largely as a spinning enterprise a century ago has now gradually developed into a mature composite industry.

The Indian Textile Industry consists of the organized textile mills on the one hand, and the decentralized power looms and handlooms on the other. The handloom industry comprises of three sectors: (1) cotton weaving, (2) wool weaving and (3) silk weaving. Of the three, cotton weaving accounts for about 90 per cent of the weaving activity in terms of number of handlooms. Thus, it happens that even today the handloom industry is the source of livelihood next only to agriculture for the largest number of Indians. There are over 30 lakh handlooms (cotton) that provide employment to about 100 lakh people on weaving alone. The production of handloom cloth is concentrated in three States, viz., Tamil Nadu, Andhra Pradesh and Uttar Pradesh. Promotion of cotton handloom industry in India is under the care of Handloom Export Promotion Council (HEPC).

Handloom Export Promotion Council

The Handloom Export Promotion Council has emerged as a highly successful agency in creating a niche for Indian Handloom

Industry in the global market. The Handloom Export Promotion Council (HEPC) acts as a liaison between the Indian exporter and the foreign importer in all matters relating to export of handloom products. Handloom Export Promotion Council has sought from the Union Government more administrative powers and financial support to meet the new challenges that have emerged due to globalisation on the export front. In order to set up promotional activities, enhanced grants under Market Development Assistance (MDA) are required for participation in fairs, organising trade delegations to other countries, launching publicity measures and conducting workshops and seminars. The Council has also called for review of the system of participating in overseas fairs through the Trade Fair Authority of India (TRAI). Apart from this, it has made several recommendations and suggestions to the government and other organizations from time to time with a view to increase exports of cotton handloom products.

Export Performance of Indian Cotton Handloom Industry

India is a country rich in traditions and cultural heritage. The spirit of swadeshi, nurtured by Mahatma, has transcended through the ages and one manifestation of it is the growth of indigenous industries, especially the Khadi and Village Industry. Handloom sector occupies a predominant place in Khadi and Village Industry. Export of handlooom products enables India to communicate to the world the value system of the Indians. The Indian handloom industry has been making a continued effort in emphasising the importance of projecting the variety of richness of the Indian fabric tradition in the world textile market.

The export performance of the handloom industry (Table 17.1) indicates that the total value of handloom exports increased from Rs. 341.45 crore to Rs. 1891.91 crore in 1999-2000. It reveals that total export earnings has increased more than five-fold in terms of value. The annual growth rate registered a maximum of 69.12 per cent in the first year of the reform process. However, the annual growth rate recorded a continuous fall after the year 1992-93 and touched a high negative growth rate of -5.78 per cent during the year 1999-2000. It may be noticed that a downward trend in the growth rate of handloom export has happened after India embraced globalisation. The persistent decline in the level of export has highly disabled the handloom sector from effectively contributing to the foreign exchange reserve of India.

Table 17.1 : Exports of Cotton Handloom Products from India: 1989-90 to 1999-2000

Year	Indian Cotton Handloom Exports (Rs.in crores)	Annual Growth Rate (in per cent)
1989-90	341.45	—
1990-91	407.29	19.28
1991-92	688.83	69.12
1992-93	1033.31	50.00
1993-94	1297.48	25.56
1994-95	1500.82	15.67
1995-96	1490.78	-0.70
1996-97	1621.81	8.78
1997-98	1854.50	14.35
1998-99	2007.90	8.27
1999-2000	1891.91	-5.78

Sources :

1. Annual Reports (1991-2000) Published by Handloom Export Promotion Council, Chennai.
2. HEPC Newsletters (1991-2000) published by Handloom Export Promotion Council, Chennai.
3. Annual Statements - Destinationwise Export of Handloom Goods published by Handloom Export Promotion Council, Chennai.

The important reason for the decline in the export growth can be attributed to the continuing recessionary trends in the world market, unprecedented escalation in the price of yarn, the restricted US quota, apart from, of course, the onslaught of liberalisation which is posing a big challenge to traditional industry like handloom.

Indian Handloom Exports : Sectoral Composition

The sectoral composition of Indian Cotton Handloom goods consists of two major product categories, viz., (i) Cotton Fabrics and (ii) Cotton Madeups. The cotton fabrics consists of Real Madras Handkerchief (RMHK), lunghies/sarangs, dhoties, sarees, shirtings, etc. The cotton madeups include floor coverings, bed-linen, table linen, towels, dish cloth, etc. Export of handloom products according to the major classification is presented in terms of quality as well as quality in Tables 17.2 and 17.3.

Table 17.2 : Exports of Indian Cotton Handloom (Quality-wise) :1991-92 to 1997-98

Year	Cotton Fabrics Exports ('000 sq.metres)	Annual Growth Rate (in per cent)	Cotton Madeups Exports ('000 kg)	Annual Growth Rate (in per cent)
1991-92	770.69	—	519.98	—
1992-93	856.51	11.14	637.00	22.55
1993-94	785.00	-8.35	790.92	24.16
1994-95	787.55	0.32	826.32	4.48
1995-96	596.32	-24.28	760.58	-7.96
1996-97	476.87	-20.03	855.14	12.43
1997-98	429.03	-10.03	882.04	3.15
1998-99	399.90	-6.79	958.65	8.69
1999-2000	400.70	0.20	926.91	-3.34

Sources :

1. *Annual Reports* (1991-2000) published by Handloom Export Promotion Council, Chennai.
2. *HEPC Newsletters* (1991-2000) published by Handloom Export Promotion Council, Chennai.
3. *Annual Statements* — Destinationwise Export of Handloom Goods published by Handloom Export Promction Council, Chennai.

Export of Cotton Fabrics

The export of cotton fabrics was 770.69 thousand square metres during the year 1992-92. After increasing by 85.82 thousand square metres in the next year, it started to decline continuously during the subsequent years which represent the post-reform era. The annual growth rate is not at all encouraging and it is heartening to note that the annual growth rates have touched high levels of

Table 17.3 : Percentage Share of Sectoral Total Composition of Indian Cotton Handloom Exports: 1989-90 to 1999-2000

Year	Cotton Fabrics (Rs.in crore)	AGR (in per cent)	Cotton Madeups Exports (Rs.in crores)	AGR (in per cent)	Total Value of Indian Cotton Exports (Rs.in crore)	AGR (in per cent)
1989-90	112.16 (32.85)	—	229.69 (67.15)	—	341.45	—
1990-91	122.66 (30.12)	9.36	284.63 (69.88)	23.92	407.29	19.28
1991-92	187.22 (27.18)	52.63	501.61 (72.82)	76.23	688.83	69.13
1992-93	272.98 (26.42)	45.80	760.29 (73.58)	51.57	1033.27	50.00
1993-94	281.59 (21.70)	3.15	1015.89 (78.30)	33.62	1297.48	25.57
1994-95	320.22 (21.34)	13.72	1180.60 (78.66)	13.95	1500.52	15.65
1995-96	254.82 (17.09)	-20.42	1235.96 (82.91)	4.95	1490.48	-0.65
1996-97	232.42 (14.33)	-8.79	1389.96 (85.67)	12.41	1621.81	8.79
1997-98	219.68 (11.85)	-5.48	1634.82 (88.15)	17.66	1854.50	14.35
1998-99	223.48 (11.13)	1.73	1784.42 (88.87)	9.16	2007.90	8.27
1999-2000	206.80 (12.27)	-7.46	1685.11 (87.73)	-5.57	1891.91	-5.78

Sources :

1. *Annual Reports* (1991-2000) published by Handloom Export Promotion Council, Chennai.
2. *HEPC Newsletters* (1991-2000) published by Handloom Export Promotion Council, Chennai.
3. *Annual Statements* — Destinationwise Export of Handloom Goods published by Export Promotion Council, Chennai.

negative values.

The total value of Indian cotton fabrics increased from Rs.112.16 crore in 1989-90 to a maximum of Rs. 320.22 crore in 1994-95. During the remaining years, it maintained a declined trend. The annual growth of total value of export earnings of cotton handloom exports was positive in the initial years of reform period and then declined registering negative values during the years 1996-97 to 1998-99. One of the prominent reasons for the poor performance of the handloom fabrics was the lack of demand for shirtings and other dress materials, predominantly due to seasonal fluctuations in the fashion market. Further a dip in the export of fabrics to USA, one of the major importers, accelerated the rate of decline in export growth.

Export of Cotton Made-ups

The cotton madeups exports, in terms of quantity, steadily increased from the year 1991-92. After a fall during the year 1995-96, it again maintained an increasing trend. While the quantity of cotton madeups exported during the year 1991-92 amounted to 519.98 thousand kilograms, it touched a whopping figure of 958.65 thousand the quantity-wise export exhibits encouraging numbers, the annual growth rate recorded in terms of percentage is not highly appealing. In fact, during two of the years (1995-96 and 1990-00) under reference, the annual growth rate touched a negative figure. The total value of export earnings of cotton madeups export increased from Rs. 229.69 crore in 1989-90 to Rs. 1784.42 crore in 1998-99. It can be observed that within 10 years, the amount of export registered a seven fold increase. The success of madeups helped handloom exports to retain its buoyancy.

Major Markets for Indian Handloom Products

Indian textile industry, one of the oldest industries, had good market for its products in the European countries in the early 18th century. However, this ancient industry was swamped by the American

Cotton and power-driven mills of Lancashire (Bedi, 1999). With the revival of the Indian textile industry in the post-independence period, the markets for the products of this industry expanded. The demand for the handloom products from the various quarters of the globe gained a momentum. At present, the important importing countries of India made handloom varieties broadly include Asian, African, European, American and Oceania regions. Country-wise exports are summarised in Tables 17.4, 17.5 and 17.6. These tables present the quantity-wise export of cotton fabrics, cotton madeups and their export earnings.

Asian Region

Indian cotton handloom (Fabrics and Madeups) exports to Asian region recorded an 86 per cent growth in terms of value and it has recorded a positive sign of growth from 1990-91 to 1994-95. Of the total exports, to Asian region, cotton fabrics exports recorded minimum of 39.45 per cent in 1997-98 and maximum of 47.81 per cent was registered in the first year of the reform process. At the same time, the annual growth rate of total quantity of cotton fabrics exports was negative in all the years, except in 1999-2000, indicating a downward trend in the goods exported.

Cotton madeups also registering the same trend as that of fabrics. The rate of growth was positive in sign in the first-three years period (1992-93 to 1994-95). Later, it became negative except in 1999-2000. This region accounted for nearly 40 per cent of total handloom fabrics exports. In the Asian region Japan has emerged as the most important importer of Indian cotton handloom products. Japanese are steady and reliable business partners. But they are very much demanding in terms of quality and consistency. The other important markets for Indian handloom goods in the Asian region are Singapore, Malaysia and the Middle East.

The freeze price competition in the Japanese market, competition from China and the economic crisis in the South East Asia, are the reasons for the drastic decline of handloom exports. The major item of export of African region is Real Madras

Table 17.4 : Major Markets for Indian Cotton (Fabrics) Handloom Exports: 1991-92 to 1999-2000 ('000 sq. metres)

Region	1991-92	1992-93	1993-94	1994-95	1995-96	1996-97	1997-98	1998-99	1999-2000
Asian Region	368.47	345.90	321.14	312.01	266.08	216.24	169.24	150.81	158.52
(Percentage share)	(47.81)	(40.38)	(40.87)	(39.62)	(44.62)	(45.38)	(39.45)	(37.71)	(39.91)
AGR (%)	—	-6.13	-7.16	-2.84	-14.72	-18.67	-21.80	-10.89	5.11
African Region	96.54	111.92	101.77	81.99	62.15	56.29	44.58	39.43	45.11
(Percentage share)	(12.53)	(13.06)	(12.95)	(10.40)	(10.42)	(11.80)	(10.39)	(9.86)	(11.28)
AGR (%)	—	15.93	-9.07	-19.44	-24.20	-9.43	-20.80	-11.55	14.41
European Region	74.79	100.46	120.23	118.50	133.47	119.96	116.53	120.07	87.40
(Percentage share)	(9.70)	(11.73)	(15.30)	(15.05)	(22.38)	(25.16)	(27.16)	(30.03)	(21.85)
AGR (%)	—	34.32	19.68	-1.44	12.63	-10.12	-2.86	3.04	-27.21
American Region	210.22	243.98	190.84	211.67	96.60	62.31	78.79	74.97	84.63
(Percentage share)	(27.28)	(28.50)	(24.29)	(26.88)	(16.20)	(13.07)	(18.36)	(18.75)	(21.15)
AGR (%)	—	16.05	21.78	10.91	-54.36	-35.50	-26.45	-4.84	12.89
Oceania Region	20.16	54.25	51.82	63.38	38.02	19.94	19.94	14.62	24.68
(Percentage share)	(2.68)	(6.34)	(6.59)	(8.05)	(6.38)	(4.19)	(4.64)	(3.65)	(6.17)
AGR (%)	—	162.45	-4.48	22.31	-40.01	-47.66	0.20	-26.68	68.88
World	770.69	856.51	785.80	787.55	596.32	476.87	429.03	399.90	400.07
	(100)	(100)	(100)	(100)	(100)	(100)	(100)	(100)	(100)
AGR (%)	—	11.14	-8.35	0.32	-24.28	-20.03	-10.03	-6.79	0.043

Sources :

1. *Annual Reports* (1991-2000) published by Handloom Export Promotion Council, Chennai.
2. *HEPC Newsletters* (1991-2000) published by Handloom Export Promotion Council, Chennai.
3. *Annual Statements* — Destinationwise Export of Handloom Goods published by Handloom Export Promotion Council, Chennai.

Table 17.5 : Major Markets for Indian Cotton (Madeups) Handloom Exports: 1991-92 to 1999-2000 ('000 kgs)

Region	1991-92	1992-93	1993-94	1994-95	1995-96	1996-97	1997-98	1998-99	1999-2000
Asian Region	68.32	87.52	151.91	175.73	141.02	110.91	110.42	93.21	101.45
(percentage share)	(13.12)	(13.75)	(19.21)	(21.27)	(18.56)	(12.97)	(12.52)	(9.72)	(10.95)
AGR (%)	—	28.27	73.57	15.68	-21.35	-12.32	-0.44	-15.59	8.84
African Region	1.05	1.92	1.32	3.46	4.59	11.04	12.99	9.29	12.86
(Percentage share)	(0.20)	(0.30)	(0.16)	(0.42)	(0.60)	(1.29)	(1.47)	(0.97)	(1.39)
AGR(%)	—	-45.31	-31.25	100.00	32.65	140.52	17.66	-26.21	38.43
European Region	180.19	233.29	298.57	298.88	259.88	344.12	368.27	449.45	457.36
(percentage share)	(34.65)	(36.62)	(37.74)	(36.17)	(34.20)	(40.24)	(41.75)	(46.88)	(49.34)
AGR (%)	—	-29.32	0.43	0.10	-13.04	32.41	7.02	22.04	1.76
American Region	240.96	268.75	301.16	308.16	308.88	334.11	342.05	367.54	321.69
(percentage share)	(46.35)	(42.18)	(38.17)	(37.29)	(40.65)	(39.07)	(38.78)	(38.34)	(34.71)
AGR (%)	—	11.53	12.31	2.10	0.23	8.17	2.38	7.45	-12.47
Oceania Region	29.55	45.55	37.29	40.09	45.41	54.96	48.28	38.46	33.55
(percentage share)	(5.68)	(7.15)	(4.72)	(4.85)	(5.99)	(6.43)	(5.48)	(4.01)	(3.62)
AGR (%)	—	54.15	18.13	7.51	13.27	21.03	-12.15	-20.34	-12.77
World	519.98	637.00	790.92	826.32	759.78	855.14	882.04	958.65	926.97
	(100.00)	(100.00)	(100.00)	(100.00)	(100.00)	(100.00)	(100.00)	(100.00)	(100.00)
AGR (%)	—	22.50	24.16	4.48	-7.96	12.43	3.15	8.69	-3.31

Sources :

1. *Annual Reports* (1991-2000) published by Handloom Export Promotion Council, Chennai.
2. *HEPC Newsletters* (1991-2000) published by Handloom Export Promotion Council, Chennai.
3. *Annual Statements* — Destinationwise Export of Handloom Goods published by Handloom Export Promotion Council, Chennai.

Table 17.6 : Percentage Share and Annual Growth of Indian Cotton Handloom Exports: 1990-91 to 1999-2000 (Rs.in crores)

Region	1990-91	1991-92	1992-93	1993-94	1994-95	1995-96	1996-97	1997-98	1998-99	1999-2000
Asian Region	88.81	164.96	220.06	313.98	377.74	363.65	290.89	391.18	247.65	242.74
(percentage share)	(21.80)	(23.83)	(21.30)	(24.30)	(24.20)	(25.71)	(17.94)	(21.1)	(12.33)	(12.83)
AGR (%)	—	86.40	33.40	42.70	20.30	-3.70	-20.00	34.50	-36.69	-1.98
African Region	24.22	28.62	42.77	42.03	41.71	37.68	44.11	43.83	38.95	42.36
(percentage share)	(5.94)	(4.13)	(4.14)	(3.24)	(2.78)	(2.53)	(2.72)	(2.4)	(1.94)	(2.24)
AGR (%)	—	18.20	49.50	1.00	-0.76	-9.70	17.10	-0.64	-11.13	8.75
European Region	130.33	193.66	314.68	415.78	204.42	517.71	682.92	720.43	942.27	878.16
(percentage share)	(32.05)	(27.97)	(30.45)	(32.05)	(33.23)	(34.73)	(42.19)	(38.80)	(46.93)	(46.42)
AGR (%)	—	48.40	62.30	32.10	21.30	2.60	6.00	15.30	30.79	-6.80
American Region	143.08	268.09	370.74	448.42	483.72	470.83	498.99	585.96	691.33	650.89
(percentage share)	(35.13)	(38.73)	(35.88)	(34.56)	(32.23)	(31.58)	(30.77)	(31.60)	(34.43)	(34.40)
AGR (%)	—	87.40	38.30	21.00	0.10	-2.70	6.00	12.40	17.98	-5.85
Oceania Region	20.63	35.89	85.06	77.26	92.23	100.92	103.43	113.43	87.71	77.76
(percentage share)	(5.06)	(5.33)	(8.23)	(5.95)	(6.21)	(6.72)	(6.38)	(6.10)	(4.36)	(4.11)
AGR (%)	—	78.60	133.00	0.90	20.70	8.20	-2.50	9.30	-22.45	-11.34
World	407.29	692.22	1033.31	1297.41	1500.82	1490.79	1621.81	1854.50	2007.90	1891.91
	(100%)	(100%)	(100%)	(100%)	(100%)	(100%)	(100%)	(100%)	(100%)	(100%)
AGR (%)	—	69.90	49.30	25.60	15.70	-0.70	8.80	14.13	8.27	-5.77

Sources :

1. *Annual Reports* (1991-2000) published by Handloom Export Promotion Council, Chennai.
2. *HEPC Newsletter* (1991-2000) published by Handloom Export Promotion Council, Chennai.
3. *Annual Statements* — Destinationwise Export of Handloom published by Handloom Export Promotion Council, Chennai.

Handkerchief (RMHK). Other items of Africa are floor-coverings, place mats and other fabrics.

African Region

The amount of exports made to countries in the African Region reveal that all along the years the value of export has remained the same. The value of exports has increased from Rs. 24.22 crore during 1990-91 to Rs. 42.36 crore during 1999-2000. Though it seems the amount had doubled, there has not been any significant increase in the rate of growth. In fact, the rate has down-tailed after the year 1992-93 during which the rate of growth was 49.50 per cent. Of the total exports, the share of the African Region remained at 5.94 per cent after which is declined. The export performance of cotton fabrics has not revealed any promising results. There has been a steady decline in the quantity of fabrics exported to the African regions. The rate of growth has remained mostly negative during all the years except 1992-93 and 1999-2000. The percentage share of the African Region in the total exports from India has covered around 10 per cent during the years from 1991-92 to 1999-2000.

Cotton fabrics export to the African Region indicated that there is no good demand for madeups from this region since the quantity of export has remained at a very low level. The annual growth rate in the export has remained highly volatile during the period. While the annual growth rate was 140.52 per cent during the year 1996-97, it was –45.31 per cent during the year 1992-93. Further, the percentage share of this region in the total export of madeups reveal that demand for madeups in this region is highly negligible.

The major countries in the African region other South Africa are Republic of Benin, Nigeria and Togoland. The decline in export is mainly due to poor economic conditions prevailing in these countries and the instability of local currencies. RMKH is an important fabric in the Nigerian way of life and is indispensable to certain rituals and customs of the people. But now trade with Nigeria is highly restrictive. Due to high incidents of duty prevailing in South Africa, exports from India could not be increased to a greater extent.

European Region

Exports to the European Region, in terms of value, has maintained impressive numbers all through the years. The amount of export stood at Rs.130.33 crore during the year 1990-91 and increased at a steady pace reaching the highest of Rs. 942.27 crore during the year 1998-99 after which it has declined marginally. The percentage share of the European Region in the total exports of handloom products has ranged between 27.97 per cent and 46.93 per cent.

Cotton fabrics export to the European Region at 47.79 thousand square metres during the year 1991-92 and increased to a height of 133.47 thousand square metres in 1995-96. The annual growth rate remained negative during three years. Compared to cotton fabrics, the export of cotton madeups exposes promising figures. There has been a constant increase in the quality of cotton fabrics exported to the European Region. During the year 1991-92 the quality of export was of the order of 180.91 thousand kilograms which increased to 457.36 thousand kilograms during the year 1999-2000. The annual growth rates are, however, not attractive.

The major importing countries of this region are U.K., Germany, France, Sweden, Italy, Netherlands, Belgium and Denmark. Germany retained its position as the largest consumer of Indian handloom goods, followed by U.K., Italy, Sweden and France. Scandinavian countries have generally provided good market for Indian Handloom goods. As Germany had passed a legislation for banning the use of AZO based dyes, in the textile items imported into that country, export of Indian handloom goods could not be increased to the desired extent. With the concept of environment friendly fabrics gaining popularity in the European countries, handloom products with their emphasis on natural fabrics, would definitely find increasing acceptance among the consumers of Europe. However the export to East European countries remain negligible.

American Region

American Regime appears to be one of the largest importers of handloom products from India. The figures of export has increased continuously from year to year except during the year 1995-96. The value of goods exported was Rs.143.08 crore during 1990-91. This increased to Rs. 650.89 crore during the year 1999-2000. The percentage share of this region in the total exports of India has ranged, between 30.77 per cent and 38.73 per cent. Export of cotton fabrics declined consistently and the annual growth rates are not encouraging. In fact during the year 1995-96, the annual growth rate registered a high negative value of -54.36 per cent.

Demand for cotton madeups in the American Region appears to be good and the quantity of madeups exported has increased from year to year, without a fall, upto the year 1998-99. During the year 1991-92, the quantity exported was of the order of 240.96 thousand kilograms and this increased to 367.54 thousand kilograms in the year 1998-99.

Madeups other than floor coverings are subject to quantitative ceilings in the U.S. In the American region, except Canada, the Indian products are still unknown, Handloom Exports Promotion Council (HEPC) had organised a business delegation to Latin America (Argentina, Brazil, Mexico). The items exported to these countries are mainly floor coverings, place mats and table cloths. It would be worthwhile to pursue the possibilities suggested by the markets of South America. Moreover, the prospects offered by the Mexican market, particularly in the context of North American Free Trade Area (NAFTA), should be explored. It is clear that to a extent the presence in the American region, new strategies and initiatives are urgently required. The main reason for the very poor performance in the export of fabrics to U.S.A. is the difficulty in setting production within the short delivery schedule stipulated by the buyers.

Oceania Region

Export of handloom products to the Oceania Region reveals that there exists a considerable demand for the Indian handloom products. The amount of export was Rs. 206.63 crores during 1990-91. The amount of exports increased year by year and touched a peak of Rs. 113.10 crores during the year 1997-98. The annual growth rates show a mixed performance in the exports since there are swings in the growth rates. It may be noted that the percentage share of the Oceania region remained around 5 per cent during the years under review.

Oceania Region seems to be less oriented towards the cotton fabrics since the quantity of export of these varieties has remained low during all the years. Further, as compared to other regions, Oceania region imports less quantity of cotton fabrics from India. The quantity exported during the year 1991-92 was 20.67 thousand square metres. After increasing for a few years, the quantity exported has again come down. The annual growth rates do not reveal any consistency.

Cotton madeups, as compared to fabrics appear to have better market in Oceania Region. Though the quality of goods exported is not encouraging, still the quantity exported continuously increasing during the first-six years. However, after this there has been a steady downtrend in the goods exported. During the last three years the annual rates of growth were negative. In the Oceania region, Australia is the leading importer of the cotton handloom products. The other main country is New Zealand. There is considerable scope for increasing the market share in these countries provided the industry offers new and attractive products at competitive rates. The main items exported to those countries are floor coverings, towels, place mats and other fabric/ madeups.

Conclusion

The Indian handloom industry is reeling under the pressure of multiple problems which may crush the export potential of this traditional sector. The capacity utilisation level has remained at low ebbs over the past few years and it is estimated that around 56 per cent of the capacity in this sector is unutilised. Obsoleteness of production technology, unwielding size of looms, increasing cost of production and lack of consistent quality of the input are but some of the problems faced by this industry. Considering the bottlenecks before this industry, the Government, both at the Centre and the State, have announced several schemes to keep this sector alive. However, it is found that despite the boost given, the industry has not gained any energy. To handle the looming threat of the handloom industry the following suggestions are offered, which if implemented in good spirit, will bail out the industry from sinking.

* Improved quality control through Research and Development Cell which may be opened by the government there is a large cluster of looms. This will enable the units to make use of good input leading to better final products.
* Innovation, which has to be the number one agenda for any manufacturer, should be pursued on a continuous basis. Better innovation becomes possible with the use of computers.
* Before starting to manufacture a product, an effort to understand what the market needs, may be undertaken. This will act as an insurance against rejection of export orders.
* In order to popularize the Indian handloom products, shops may be opened at spots wherein foreign nationals visit in large number. For instance, outlets dealing with handloom goods may be opened in places of tourists' importance. Further handloom product outlets may be opened in international airports of various countries.
* Whenever foreign delegates pay a visit to Indian on any purpose, they may be offered a good variety of handloom products as a bouquet. After all, a satisfied customer is a good advertisement.
* In the era of globalisation, resorting to interest becomes indispensable to create connectivity with the buyer. In this direction, the manufactures of the handloom sector may create a web describing the features of their product. This is sure to fetch more number of importers.

To export successfully in a global economy is to get integrated into it. Globalisation is not a simple process of integration with World market *via* arm's length market transactions. Countries are incorporated in the global economy through a network of international production, trade and finance. The design of reform policies which facilitate India's participation in the global network of production needs greater attention. The key to success in the international market place seems to be the attitude, "I will make what you need and not I will sell what I make".

References

Annual Statements, Destinationwise exports of Handloom Goods (various issues: 1991-2000), published by Handloom Promotional Council, Chennai.

Bedi, C.S. (1999) *General Studies,* S. Chand & Company Ltd., New Delhi.

Datt Ruddar and Sundaram, K.P.M. (2000) *Indian Economy*, S. Chand & Company, New Delhi.

Handloom Export Promotion Council News Letters (1991-99) Published by Handloom Promotion Exports Council, Chennai.

Handloom Export Promotion Council (1991-99) *Annual Reports*, Published by Handloom Exports Council, Chennai.

Kothari Industrial Directory (1996) Published by Kothari Groups of Companies, Chennai.

Ramasamy, K.V. (2000) *Exporting in Globalised Economy*, in Indian Development Report.

Rizwanual Islam (1996) "Economic Reforms, Employment and Labour Market in South Asia", *Indian Journal of Labour Economics,* Vol. 39, No. 3, July-September.

Sudha Deshpande and L.K. Deshpande (1996) "Impact of Liberalisation on Labour Market and Industrial Relations in India, *Indian Journal of Labour Economics,* Vol. 39, No. 3, July-September.

18

CONSUMER'S BEHAVIOUR TOWARDS HANDLOOM TEXTILE : A Study

— *R. Karunakaran* and *M. Karthikeyan*

"A customer is the most important visitor on our premises. He is not dependent on us. We are dependent on him. He is not an interruption on our work. He is not an outsider on our business. He is a part of it. We are doing him a favour by serving him. He is doing us a favour by giving us an opportunity to do so."

— *Mahatma Gandhiji.*

Introduction

Handloom Weavers Cooperatives are basically manufacturing organisations. They procure necessary raw materials and other inputs from various suppliers and convert them into finished products with the combined efforts of other production factors such as man, machine and money. Management of handloom weaver's cooperatives assumes greater significance and the accomplishment of the ultimate object of societies depends on how the outputs are matched with the market. Therefore the management of such cooperative should draw their responsibilities from the consumers, as they are the actual patrons of the society. The whole of output is to be sold in the market otherwise it will be serious problem to the organisation. What consumers need is to be produced? And accordingly all the activities with regard to production, pricing, distribution and promotion are to be framed and carried on.

To understand about consumer's market the following Questions such as Who is in the market? What does the market buy? When does the market and the like is more helpful to any marketer. In addition to these, the relationship between the marketing stimuli and consumer response is also to be understood. To have thorough understanding about the market, the demand, the competitors, the behaviour of consumers, a field level consumer survey is of most avail. Today in Tamil Nadu, weavers cooperatives are facing a number of problems; stock piles up; year after year sales started declining; large number of societies become dormant and defunct; large number of member weavers are thrown away from continuous employment; societies are unable to provide continuous employment to their members. As answers to all such problems, understanding about the consumers (consumer markets) and their behaviour towards handloom products are *sine-qua-non*. Here is an attempt at micro level and hence this study.

The following are the objectives of this study :

1. To study the nature and extent of use of handloom fabrics,
2. To analyse the factors influencing the buying behaviour of consumers, and
3. To find out the post-purchases behaviour towards handloom fabrics.

As this study attempts to gather data from the field, survey method was adopted. Sanarpatty village, Natham Taluk, Dindigul district was selected purposively as the area for this study. Adopting simple random sampling procedure selection of the respondents were done. Thus total hundred household respondents formed the populous of the study. As this study required field data (primary data) from the individual respondents, personal interview technique was employed.

Consumer's Behaviour

"Buying behaviour is all psychological social and physical behaviours of potential consumers as they become aware of to evaluate, purchase, consume and tell other people about products and services."

Buyer behaviours emphasizes that this behaviour is both individual processes and group processes :

(a) The psychological needs, which includes needs for satisfying hunger, thirst, sleep, shelter and sex gratification.
(b) The safety needs are related to economic and social security such as economic security, protection and family security.
(c) The belongings and love needs need to be satisfied to avoid frustration and maladjustments in life.
(d) The esteem needs comprise esteem needs a high evaluation of others in society.
(e) The need for self-actualisation is the desire to achieve the maximum of one's capabilities.
(f) The desire to know and understand refers to the process of reaching for meaning in things around us.
(g) The aesthetic needs which may not appear to be present among many individuals because of their failure to satisfy more basic needs, but among others the need for beauty is important.

In earlier times, marketers could arrive at a fair understanding of consumers through the daily experience of selling to them. But the size of firms and markets has removed many marketing decision-makers from direct contact with their customers. Increasingly, managers have had to turn to consumer research. They are spending more money than ever to study consumers, trying to learn who buys? Why do they buy?

Of central interest is the question, How do consumers respond to various marketing stimuli that the company might arrange? The company that really understands how consumers will respond to different product features, prices advertising appeals, and so on, will have an enormous advantage over its competitions. The stimuli on the left are of two types. Marketing stimuli consist of the four P's — product, price, place and promotion.

Other stimuli consist of major forces and event in the buyer's environments, economic, technological, political and cultural.

Outside stimuli		Buyer's black box	
Marketing	Other		
Product Price Place Promotion	Economic Technological Political Cultural	Buyer Characteristics	Buyer Decision Process
Buyer's responses			
Product	Choice		
Brand	Choice		
Dealer	Choice		
Purchase	Timing		
Purchase	Amount		

Their starting point is the stimulus response model shown in Figure shows marketing and other stimuli entering the buyers "black box" and producing certain responses.

The marketer's task is to understand what happens in the buyer's black box between the stimuli and responses. The buyer's black box has two components :

(1) The buyer's characteristics have a major influence on how he or she reacts to the stimuli.

(2) The buyer's decision process influences the outcome.

Major Factors Influencing Consumers Behaviours

Consumer does not make their decisions in a vacuum. Their purchase is highly influenced by culture, social, personal and psychological factors.

Cultural Factors

Cultural factors exert the broadest and deepest influence on consumer behaviour. We will look at the role played by the buyer's culture, sub-culture and social class.

Culture : Culture is the most fundamental determinant of a person's wants and behaviour. Whereas lower creatures are largely governed by instinct, human behaviours is largely learned. The child growing up in a society learns a basic set of values, perceptions, preferences, and behaviours through process of socialization involving the family and other key institutions.

(i) Sub-culture : Each culture contains smaller groups of sub-cultures that provide more specific identification and socialisation for its members. Four types of sub-cultures can be distinguished.

(a) *Nationality groups:* Such as the Irish, Polish, Italians and Puerto Ricans are found within large communities and exhibit distinct tastes and proclivities.
(b) *Religious groups:* Such as the Catholics, Mormons, Presbyterians and Jews represent sub-cultures with specific cultural preferences and taboos.
(c) *Racial groups:* Such as Blacks and Orientals have distinct cultural styles and attitudes.
(d) *Geographical areas:* Such as the Deep south, California and New England are distinct sub-cultures with characteristic life style.

(ii) Social class : Virtually all human societies exhibit social stratification, stratification sometimes takes the form of a caste system when the members of different castes are reared for certain roles and cannot change their caste membership. Social classes are relatively homogeneous and enduring division in a society,

which are hierarchically ordered, and whose members share similar values interests and behaviours.

Social Factors

A consumer's behaviour is also influenced by social factors, such as the consumer's reference groups, family and social roles and statuses.

(i) Reference groups : A person's behaviour is strongly influenced by many groups. A person's reference groups are those that have a direct (face-to-face) or indirect influence on the person's attitudes or behaviour. Groups having a direct influence on a person are called membership groups. These are groups to which the person belongs and interacts. Some are primary groups with which there is fairly continuous interaction, such as family, friends, neighbours and co-workers. Primary groups tend to be informal. The person also belongs to secondary groups, which tend to be more formal and where there is less continuous interaction. They include religious organisations, professional association, and trade unions.

(ii) Family : Members of the buyers of the buyer's family can exercise a strong influence on the buyer's behaviour. We can distinguish between two families in the buyer's life. The family of orientation consists of one's parents. From parents a person acquires an orientation toward religion, politics, and economic and a sense of personal ambition, self-worth and live. Even if the buyer no longer interacts very much with his or her parents the parent's influence on the unconscious behaviours of the buyer can be significant. In countries where parents continue to live with their children, their influence can be substantial.

A more direct influence on every day buying behaviours is one's family of procreation, namely one's spouse and children. The family is the most important consumer-buying organisation in a society, and it has been researched extensively. Marketers are interested in the roles and relative influence of the husband, wife and children in the purchase of a large variety of products and services.

(iii) Roles and statuses : A person participates in many groups throughout life—family clubs, organisations. The persons' position in each group can be defined in terms of role and status. A role consists of the activities that a person is expected to perform according to the persons around him or her.

Each of day's roles will influence some of his buying behaviour.

Each role carries a status reflecting the general esteem accorded to it by society. People often choose products to communicate their role and status in society.

Personal Factors

A buyer's decisions are also influenced by his or her personal characteristics, notably the buyer's age and life cycle stage, occupation, economic circumstances, life style and personality and self-concept.

(i) Age and life cycle stage : People change the goods and services they buy over their life time. Consumption is also shaped by the stage of the family life cycle.

(ii) Occupation : A person's consumption pattern is also influenced by his or her occupation. Blue-colour wormers will buy work clothes, work shoes, lunch boxes, and bowling recreation.

(iii) Economic circumstances : A person's economic circumstances will greatly affect product choice. People's economic circumstances consist of their spendable income, savings and assets, borrowing power, and attitude towards spending *versus* saving.

(iv) Life-Style : People coming from the same sub-culture, social classes and even occupation may lead quite different life styles. A person's life style, then in the person's pattern of living in the world

as expressed in the person's activities, interest and opinions life style reflects one thing beyond the person's social class, on the one hand or personality on the other.

(v) Personality and Self-Concept : Each person has a distinct personality, that will influence his or her buying behaviour. Personality can be useful and valuable in analysing consumer behaviour provided personality type can be classified. A person's personality is usually described in terms of such traits as self-confidence. Many marketers use a concept related to personality of a person's self-concept or self-image.

Psychological Factors

"A person's buying choices are also influenced by four major psychological factors — motivation, perception, learning, and beliefs and attitudes."

(i) Motivation : A motive is a need that is sufficiently pressing to direct the person to seek satisfaction of the need.
(ii) Perception : A motivated person is ready to act. How the motivated person acts is influenced by his or her perception of the situation. Perception can be defined as "The process by which an individual selects, organises, and interprets information input to create a meaningful picture of the world.
(iii) Learning : Learning describes changes in an individual's behaviours arising from experience.
(iv) Belief and attitudes : A belief is a descriptive throughout that a person holds about something.

Decision Making Process in buying

This process consists of five steps, viz., (i) recognition of the unsatisfied needs, (ii) identification of alternative ways of reducing tensions (iii) evaluation of alternatives available, (iv) purchase decision and (v) post-purchase behaviour.

(i) Recognition of unsatisfied needs : An unsatisfied needs usually leads to tension. Such need is recognised either through advertisement or the sight of the product. When once the need is recognised conflict develops as to how competitive needs may be satisfied. Therefore, conflicts must be resolved.

(ii) Identification of alternatives : The consumer's should know that different alternatives and products are available so that the needs could be satisfied in a better way.

(iii) Evaluation of alternatives : Having identified the various alternatives the consumer must evaluate each alternative. His past experience and his attitudes towards various brands or opinion of the members of his family would enable him to evaluate the various alternatives.

(iv) Purchase decision : At this stage the consumer is to decide whether at all he is going to purchase the product to satisfy his needs. "This he will consider with reference to the product, type, brand, price, quality or colour." The seller can by making specific advertisements enable the consumer to make decisions in these matters.

(v) Post-purchase behaviour : "Buyer's feelings and evaluation after the sale are significant for the marketing management because they can influence repeat sales and also influence what the buyer tells others about the product or brand."

Major Findings

I. *Socio-Economic Variables*

* A majority (78%) of the respondents conducted for this study were males and the remaining were females.
* Only 13 per cent of the respondents were illiterate and of the literate, a majority 73 per cent of the respondents were having

primary, middle and high school level of educational status.

* Excepting 12 per cent all the respondents were belonging to backward (42%) and scheduled castes, scheduled tribes (46%).
* A high majority (96%) of the respondents belong of Hindu religion followed by Muslim 2 per cent and Christian 2 per cent.
* A majority (85%) of the respondents were married. Among the family persons, a majority 43 per cent was falling under II and III state. Categorization of Fullest as I, II and III was done primarily based on a number of dependents (children) of the respondents.
* Majority (57%) of the respondents have joint family and remaining 43 per cent of the respondents have nuclear family.
* Majority (42%) of the respondents have small size family (upto 4), 41 per cent of the respondents have medium size family (5-8) and remaining 17 per cent of the respondents have large size family (above 8).
* Majority (80%) of the respondents were employed and excepting 8 per cent, the remaining 12 per cent are employers primarily agriculturists. The reasons for large proportion of employees among the respondents was due to demand for labour created by the local industries.
* Majority (81%) of the respondents have agriculture as their main occupation, 19 per cent of the respondents have other than agriculture. A majority 70 per cent of the respondents has subsidiary occupation, such as dairying, sheep rearing etc.
* Majority (52%) of the respondents was unskilled workers followed by skilled 46 per cent and profesional vocations being just 2 per cent.
* Majority (46%) of the respondents was belonged low-income group and to percentage under high-income group belongs very insignificant.

II. Buying Behaviour Towards Textiles

Consumption of Fabrics

Majority of the respondents were using cotton fabrics of the man-made and the respondents using other than cotton fabrics such as silk, polyester, art silk etc., preferred mill-made.

Consumption Discrimination

The respondents who purchase fabrics for his own, purchased man made cotton textiles and if it was for wife alone man made polyester textile were purchased and if it was for children alone mill made polyester fabrics were bought and used.

Extent of Consumption

Majority of the respondents used man made textile of both cotton and polyester fabrics for their entire requirements.

III. Behaviour Towards Handloom Fabrics

Factors considered while buying Handloom textiles

Majority of them preferred medium quality, price and finesse handloom textiles than low or high levels.

Colour Preferences

With regard to colour preference of handloom textiles 16 per cent of the respondents preferred to purchase dark and light in plain colour followed by 42 per cent on plain colour.

Design Preference

As far as design of the handloom textile, a single majority 48 per cent of the respondents preferred and considered combination of all designs followed by 6 per cent on built weaving designs.

Skin Complexion Consideration

Large number of respondents preferred both dark contrast as well as light contrast matching colours.

Other Factors that are considered while buying

Domestic usage, social acceptance and relative competence were the factors considered more than other factors while buying handloom textiles.

Extent of Use of Handloom Fabrics

The respondents were using handloom fabrics regularly was more than the seasonal and occasional users. Hardcore was more for dhotis, towels, lungis and sarees whereas softcores were more for shirting and suiting, sarees and bed sheets.

IV. Buying Decisions

Influence of Persons on Buying Decision

Among the influential person wife/husband, children and parents played a significant role than others. Wife/husband was influencing much while buying cotton and silk handloom fabrics and children for polyester handloom fabrics.

Time of Purchase of Handloom Textile

Majority (65%) of the respondents purchased handloom fabrics during the month from January to March followed by 48 per cent during the month from October to December.

V. Post-purchase Behaviour Towards Handloom Textiles, Post-purchase Behaviour (Cotton)

An average of 10.67 per cent, 70 per cent and 7 per cent of the respondents were not satisfied, satisfied and highly satisfied with regard to handloom cotton fabrics after use respectively. The percentage of respondents satisfied with handloom cotton textiles of all items was very high.

Post-purchase Behaviour (Polyester)

With regard to polyester handloom fabrics a majority (67.5%) of the respondents were satisfied and only 9 per cent were not satisfied. And the proportion of respondents satisfied with polyester handloom dhotis and sarees were higher than any other polyester item.

Post-purchase Behaviour (Silk)

With regard to handloom silk fabrics of dhotis, sarees shirting/suiting majority of the respondents who used them were satisfied in the product and the percentage of respondents under not-satisfied category being very small.

VI. Post-purchase Behaviours (product attributewise)

Majority (more than 70%) of the respondents were satisfied with the product attributes such as quality, durability, design, colour, price and variety of the handloom fabrics and the percentage of respondents under not-satisfied category being very minimum.

Study of consumer's behaviours towards handloom textiles is nothing but a market survey, which enables handloom industry to increase its productivity and profitability. From this study, it may be concluded that majority of the respondents under-explained their views in a satisfied manner with regard to pre-purchase and post-purchase behaviour. Further, it may be stated that among handloom products cotton fabrics have always greater demand in the market compared to other handloom products such as polyester and silk fabrics.

References

Akurathi Venkateswara Rao, K., 1983, "The Handloom Sector", *The Cooperator,* 21(3), August.

Gangadhara Rao & Suryaprakasa Rao,1987, "Comparing Rural Unemployment through Rural Industrialisation", *Kurushetra,* 36(2), October.

Philip, Kotler, 1983, *Marketing Management,* New Delhi, Prentice Hall of India.

Philip, Kolter, 1997, *Principles of Marketing,* New Delhi, Prentice Hall of India.

Rao, K K & Shanmugasundaram, A.P., 1985, "Utilisation of Weavers Cooperative Society by members — A case study", *Indian Co-operative Review,* 18(2), January.

Rayudu, C.S. 1982, "Marketing aspect of Handloom Cooperatives", *The Cooperator,* 20 (2), July.

ANNEXURE

Table 18.1 : Post-purchase behaviour (Cotton)

Sl. No.	Category	No. of Respondents		
		NS	S	HS
1.	Dhotis/Lungis	20	75	5
2.	Sarees	14	81	3
3.	Shirting	10	78	5
4.	Suiting	8	50	3
5.	Ready mades	4	64	6
6.	Bed sheets	8	72	20
Average		10.67	70	7

Table 18.2 : Post-purchase behaviour (Polyester)

Sl. No.	Category	No. of Respondents		
		NS	S	HS
1.	Dhotis	16	71	2
2.	Sarees	6	82	5
3.	Shirting	9	65	10
4.	Ready mades	5	52	14
	Average	9.0	67.5	7.75

Table 18.3 : Post-purchase behaviour (Silk)

Sl. No.	Category	No. of Respondents		
		NS	S	HS
1.	Dhotis	11	21	2
2.	Sarees	2	19	5
3.	Shirting	4	16	3
	Average	5.67	9.33	3.33

Table 18.4 : Post-purchase behaviours (Product attributeswise)

Sl. No.	Category	No. of Respondents		
		NS	S	HS
1.	Quality	21	62	9
2.	Durability	12	73	15
3.	Design	11	79	9
4.	Colour	10	84	2
5.	Price	17	79	4
6.	Variety	10	75	15

(Multiple replies were received)

19

WOMEN AND RURAL INDUSTRIALISATION : Problems and Prospects

— *G. Uma Shankar* and *G. Uma*

Women who make half of the world's population can no more remain as ornamental decorative pieces but a productive human resource and recognised as such with all their entitlements. The concept of empowerment of women is gaining currency in the recent years. It refers to entrepreneurial self-reliance. The core of women empowerment framework can be viewed in terms of five levels of equality. Of which empowerment is an essential element at each level. The levels are welfare, access, conscientisation, participation and control. The existing statistics states that, women's sex ratio, educational levels, health standards, maternal mortality rate, infant mortality rate and employment levels continue to be in deplorable state. This seems to be in two different extremes. When the indicators are used in two conditions such as the rural and urban.

The development of women will be of a dream for ever unless they are made economically independent and educated. Women are not provided with their basic minimum requirements as they are bonded with economic emancipation of women will be made effective with the process of rural industrialisation. As rural industrialisation is the only best alternative available to make the women empowered and stimulate the process of sustainable development. Since India is a country of villages and large parts of its population reside in the villages and so rural industrialisation will serve to the needs of the human resources and other renewable and non-renewable resources to achieve the desired ends.

Why Women

In general women are least bothered in many walks of life. Especially in education health and employment. Their condition seems to be deploring day by day. Women form not only half of the population, produce half of the food supply, account for sixty percent of the working force, contribute up to 33.3 per cent of the official labour force, perform nearly 66.6 per cent of all working hours, receive 10 per cent of the economy but surprisingly own less than 1 per cent of the real estate. This states the status of women today. Secondly, the human race has undergone two great waves of change, each one largely obliterating earlier culture of civilisation and replacing them with the ways of life in conceivable to those who came before. The first wave of change, the agricultural revolution took thousands of years to play itself out. The second wave, the rise of industrial civilisation took a more than three hundred years. Today history is even more accelerative and it is likely that the third wave will sweep across history and complete; itself in a few decades.

Tearing our families apart, rocking our economy, paralysing our political system, shattering our values and thus the third wave will affect everyone. Yes the first two waves have made women totally out of the mainstream and worsened their condition. The status was deploring and so an alternative has to be sought.

Thirdly, the experiences of status of life of women especially in the rural areas can be expressed as —

POOR STATUS OF LIFE

↓

POOR EMPLOYMENT POTENTIAL AND OPPORTUNITY

↓ ↓

POOR STANDARD OF LIVING → POOR NUTRITION AND HEALTH

POOR INCOME

Poor status and standard of living includes the social economical, political, cultural and educational dimensions of life of women.

Fourthly, women are more honest, committed, sincere, dedicated and God fearing than their male counterparts, hence they are denied of their basic rights.

Fifthly, women role is totally neglected in resource utilisation in the rural areas. Hence we experience under-development. This is expressed as

Quantity and Quality Resources
↓
Improper maintenance and preservation
↓
Discriminated sharing
↓
Unifaceted development
↓
Socio-Economic conflicts
↓
Under-development
↓
Poor Utilisation of Resources

Sixthly, women labour force is not properly utilised.

This is shown as

S. No.	Category	Urban	Rural
1.	Male	48.92	52.58
2.	Female	9.19	26.79

Source : Computed.

Seventhly, women are hard, rational and multifaceted decision makers, but they are not utilised properly.

As the educational status is poor women are ignorant and dependent.

In practice today we are at a historic moment, in which the ideologies have died and for her there is no messiah and mankind finds itself alone with its responsibility. We cann't think about great queries and great solution, We have to solve the concrete problems and investigate the small solutions. But to the extent that these problems are caused by this system. They cannot be solved with its own logic and they do not have small solutions. These are concrete problems. We require great solutions, new approaches, dynamic and new perspectives. Thus when we talk about the economic emancipation of women we must answer to this question.

The central diseases of Indian poverty and ignorance can be removed by making the women economically empowered.

The existing socio-economic conflicts in the rural areas can be resolved by empowering women.

Complemention of women can make to run to the maximum extent possible and make herself equal and contribute the best for the betterment of the society where she is a part.

Development is possible when made to involve in all the stages of the process.

Women are made victims of the violence of different kinds and it effects their life in such a way that they cannot come out the clutches of social bondages. Thus this social bondage has to be broken down.

The salvation of this country is mainly based on the status of women.

Hence against this background only the concept of women and rural industrialisation is looked in and the outcome are explained in the following paragraphs.

Women and Rural Industrialisation

Development and prosperity is not possible unless half of the population are neglected from the mainstream of the process. Thus women as a group have a better capacity to carry the collective, because they have a realistic appraisal of life. Simply put they are better mobilisers. This is true when we undergo an analysis on the women headed institutions. In practice as far as rural areas are concerned women are still in the primitive stage or in a old prison. Here and there we could find one or two exceptions. But exceptions cannot be taken for granted.

Rural industrialisations viewed in a broader sense and the other classifications made in this category can be called as small scale industries including food processing industries and khadi village and cottage industries. The aim of making the women to involve in the process of rural industrialisation is to make them as bread winners out of being mere wives.

The Problems

The concept of women development and women empowerment is having a long cherished history and success are attained by many women though they face a series of problems. In particular when women are concerned about rural industrialisation process, the problems listed here comes into the stream.

— Difficulty in finding a space for establishment.
— Difficulty in tracing there resources.
— Lack of research.

— Lack of technical know-how.
— Lack of skilled labour force.
— Lack of investment.
— Ignorance on higher side among the rural women on rural entrepreneurship.
— Majority of the existing industries are facing the dooms and hence they have created as sense of fear among women not to engage in initiative in industrial sector.
— Problems associated with market facilities and potentials.
— Lack of encouragement

It is wise to conclude that these problems alone makes the women not to be out of the process. No, there are several other issues that which are closely associated in the process. They are called as major issues affecting the women entrepreneurship. The identified issues are :

1. Female foeticide
2. Female infanticide
3. Malnutrition
4. Domestic harassment
5. No consideration of feelings
6. Sexual harassment in workplaces
7. Gender discrimination
8. Education beyond primary level for women
9. Denial of technical education
10. Dual responsibility both in home and working place
11. Sexual exploitations
12. Increasing work load
13. Denial of basic amenities in working place
14. Lack of health facilities
15. Food habits
16. Lack of medical care
17. Domestic situations
    Drinking water
    Fuel wood

Public distribution system
Child care results in tension

18. Facing to have sex against their will
19. Liquor consumption
20. Viewing women as a child bearing machine
21. Denial of property — non-information of law
22. Made women victims of different kinds of violences
23. No security in unorganised sector
24. Widow remarriage is still a dream
25. Menstrual syndrome
26. Wage differences
27. Over-workload less wage
28. Employed in hazardous industries
29. Total dependence
30. A notion is there that the work done by women are easy
31. Voting rights are denied
32. Name sake participation alone is allowed in political activities
33. Not easy to form an organisation or association
34. Very difficult to approach the political leaders
35. Character assassination
36. When women enter into politics, they are not considered as leaders, they are treated as proxies
37. Judiciary is still conservative. Judgments are mostly based on the Judges
38. Women's rights are still in papers only.

The above said issues and problems are caused due to the following factors ruling on the rural women on a major part.

Inadequate supply of information, skill and capacity
Domination of male members
Poor in communication
Poor in mobilisation
Increasing domestic workload
Unaware of the facilities, programmes, projects and schemes
Unaware of the importance of human resource and its potential

Complicative procedures in banking and other agencies
Not conscious of their self.

Thus because of the ruling of these said factors women in the rural areas find it very hard to make themselves to be out of the social and cultural bondages and get themselves in the process of development. It is vital to make a note that women's role in the process of rural industrialisation has its own significance.

The Prospects

One of the best alternative available today to make the women economically independent and make them as full-fledged citizens are rural industries. These rural industries don't require huge capital of money, material and man (woman). The appropriate technology and optimum utilisation of locally available resources can make the process to start with and proceed in a right direction. The expectation can be stated as

Quality and quantity resources

Optimum utilisation and proper preservation

Increased employment potential and opportunity

High income

Good standard of living

Higher status of life

Sustainable Development and harmony

Women and their role in rural industrialisation will result in the achievement of the following milestones :

* Proper identification and utilisation of all kinds of resources.
* Proper preservative measures for future use.
* Diversified action leads to multifaceted growth.
* Social change takes place in a rapid way.

* Growth, change and development of various industries becomes inevitable
* Reduction in poverty
* Removal of social evils.
* Utilisation of human resource in proper direction leads to the development of the human resource.
* Social justice can be achieved easily.

Thus we have found that the role of women in the context of rural industrialisation is totally inevitable and it the only available alternative key to achieve development, prosperity and harmony. Is this possible all of a sudden and can it happen or takes place on its own? No, yet another alternative or arrangement has to be made and followed. The first step can be sensitisation of women. Educating the women and making them aware of the importance of their role and functions in the context of development. Hence we can start with the process by orienting the women. The orientation process can be done by NGO's, Educational Institutions, Families, women organisations etc. This orientation has to include the planning component into it. Secondly, they are in need of a supportive organisation, information, periodical sensitisation and training. Thus by making these components available to women, we can change the existing rural situation and achieve the primary aim of rural development.

Conclusion

The ultimate aim of any activity or programme is to attain development in a more sustainable way. So is the concept women and rural industrialisation. Here one should not forget the primary objective that there are very many hurdles in the process but those can be removed by creating awareness and this awareness will lead to gain of knowledge and skill development, in turn this will result in attitudinal and behavioural change leading to development at the final stage. Yet another aspect to me taken into account is that there are schemes and programmes exclusively meant for women from both the central and State government and the one who initiates the process must take this as a primary concern. Hence with a multi-dimensional and integrated effort we can make the process of rural industrialisation more prosperous by making women equal to take part in it and ultimately achieve prosperity and harmony to the country of which we are proud.

References

Nilavalam, April 1999.

Outlook, special number on Women.

Palanithurai, G (ed). *Contemporary Issues in Development Dynamics,* Kanishka Publishers, New Delhi, 1998.

Palanithurai, G., *New Panchayati Raj System: Issues and Prospects,* Kanishka Publishers, New Delhi, 1996.

Rural Industrialisation in India, Government of India Report, 1996.

Shanthi, K. (ed) *Empowerment of Women,* Anmol Publications P. Ltd., New Delhi, 1998.

Soundarapandian, M., *Industrial Resurgence in Rural India*, Kanishka Publishers, New Delhi, 2000.

Srivastava, S.R., *A Practical Guide to Industrial Entrepreneurs,* Sultan Chand & Sons, New Delhi, 1996.

The Hindu, January 3, 1994, Madurai.

The Hindu, January 11, 1999, Madurai.

Thittam, March 1999.

Thittam, March 2000.

20

WOMEN ENTREPRENEURS FOR RURAL INDUSTRIALISATION

— *N. Nagesh Kumari* and *C. Renuka*

Introduction

Rural industries consitute the backbone of a developing country like India, occupying a commanding height in the strategy of development. These industries have become an invaluable weapon in bringing to fruition a balanced, integrated and egalitarian socio-economic order in our country.

By utilising fruitfully the technical know-how and other forms of tangible aid offered generously by industrially advanced countries like West Germany, the USA, the UK and the USSR, advanturous entrepreneurs have made an impressive progress in developing this vital sector of national economy.

The basic objectives underlying the development of rural industries are the increase in the supply of manufactured goods, the promotion of capital formation, the development of indigenous entrepreneurial talents and skills and the creation of employment opportunities. Rural industries constitute the key link in the process of socio-economic transformation of underdevelopment social structures.

Out of the total industrial employment in the country, about 80 per cent is provided by village and cottage industries. If the rural industries are well managed, rapid economic development will be possible in the country.

Women Entrepreneurs

The world today is looking for entrepreneurs who are :

Honest
Enthusiastic
Innovative
Hard working
Motivating
Optimistic

It is found that women do possess these traits somewhat in greater quantum than men. Hence, one must be optimistic to visualise a prosperous tomorrow for women entrepreneurship in a developing country like ours. Entrepreneurship among women is a recent phenomenon. Therefore it is desirable that first generation entrepreneurs with their limited financial resources and experience should go in for small and rural industries. Today we find women in different types of industries, traditional as well as non-traditional, from engineering and electronics to doll-making and poultry.

SWOT Analysis on Women Entrepreneurs

Strengths

* Commitment and dedication to the enterprise.
* Planned and systematic approach.
* Family support.
* Scarifice and hardwork of women have been declared as cross-culturally validated entrepreneurial qualities.

Weaknesses

* Lack of confidence and motivation.

* Not being able to take calculated risks because of their nurturing nature.
* The enterprise taking second place to home.
* Idea generation will also be lesser as they could not interact with many.
* Lack of information regarding how to go about formulating a business plan starting first with a market survey, project finalisation and so on.
* Lack of knowledge about the available opportunities - information about procedures and sources of assistance in setting up a business including raising finance, legal formalities etc.
* Lack of knowledge about managing the enterprise. This includes areas like accounting, marketing handling people and so on.
* Problems is offering the margin money and guarantors to avail the institutional finance.
* Marketing is another weak area for women entrepreneurs.

Opportunities

* Increasing societal concern with gender equality.
* Government policies to improve female status.
* Educational background.

Threats

* Competition from small and big units.
* Necessity of having to give up enterprise due to family reasons.
* The threat from the negative outcome of government economic policies.

Women Entrepreneurship in India

Rural Indian economy is most suited to the growth of small business has a far better scope for women entrepreneurship particularly in villages.

Women entrepreneurship is relatively a recent phenomenon in India which came into prominence in the late 1970s. According to an estimate, there were roughly three lakh women entrepreneurs sharing only 11.2 per cent of total entrepreneurs in India in 1995-96. In the case of small manufacturing units, nearly 8 per cent are run exclusively by women entrepreneurs. Although the number of women entrepreneurs is on the increase proportionately it is small in comparison with the developed countries of the world.

Most of the women entrepreneurs in India are in the informal sector, the constituents of which include agro-processing industries, food processing, readymade garments, plastic goods, making pickles and readymade masalas, printing, leather goods, hotels and restaurants, trading in wholesale and retail in finished goods and fruits and vegetables, services like beauty parlours and laundry services, embroidery, making greeting cards etc.

Entrepreneurial activity is disproportionately low due to certain constraints and taboos in the Indian society. The task of women entrepreneurship is full of challenges. They have to encounter public criticism, family prejudices and opposition and social constraints in the process of emerging as entrepreneurs. The process of urbanisation provides an impetus to women entrepreneurship in India. Ruralites are comparatively slow in accepting entrepreneurial activities due to certain inhibitions. However recent trends show that women in semi-urban and rural areas have also started picking up the entrepreneurial activities.

Rural India comprising nearly six lakh and odd villages offers a vast scope for women entrepreneurial ventures.

Women Entrepreneurs in Rural Industries

For the development of rural industries there should be a comprehensive, integrated approach. The authorities responsible for development of rural industries must take action simultaneously on the various components of the programmes especially in the case of women entrepreneurs, including

1. Identification of opportunities for rural industries
2. Financial support
3. Technical assistance
4. Entrepreneurial skills
5. Marketing support
6. Advisory services
7. Procedures to facilitate procurement of quality raw material and equipment
8. Entrepreneurship development
9. Industrial training and development administration

It is concluded that with the above comprehensive approach, women can prove their success in the field of rural industries through proper guidance and assistance. The women entrepreneurship development in the small sector particularly in villages can integrate them in the economic development of the country.

References

Dahia, L. N., "Emerging profile of women entrepreneurs and workers in India", *Southern Economist,* August 1, 2000.

Desai, Vasant, *Entrepreneurial Development,* vol. 1, 1991.

Dilip, M., Sarawate, *Entrepreneurial Development — Concept and Practices,* Himalaya Publishing House, New Delhi, 1996.

Kowshik, Madhulika, Entrepreneurial competencies and genderwise variation, *Women in Management - Champions of Change,* Khair Jahan Sogra (Ed.), University Press Ltd., Dhaka, Bangla Desh, 1994.

Umesh, Usha, "Women Entrepreneurs in the informal sector — Study of Kerala, *Southern Economist,* December 1&15, 1999.

21

ROLE OF KVIC IN PROMOTING KHADI AND VILLAGE INDUSTRIES

— *M. Soundarapandian* and *S. Palanivel*

Introduction

Cottage industries can be the most sophisticated and it has been, town based rather than village based. In fact, the old Indian cities of Benaras and Jaipur had been traditional homes of world famous crafts. Gold and silk brocades from Benaras and the jewellery from Jaipur were known in the best markets of the world. But today the role of the cottage industry, at least, potentially is far more important for the villages than for the cities and towns. This is because, on the one hand modern industry has taken over the urban sector; on the other hand, village industries alone can retain the agriculturist in agriculture, and at the same time, remove some part of the disguised and seasonal unemployment that he has to face in agriculture.

Poverty and its associated phenomena the hunger, illiteracy and high birth rates pervade, in spite of gains in self-sufficiency in food spread, education and family welfare programmes. In short, we are called upon to face the challenge of economic development with social justice at its end. The sheer number of hands clamouring for jobs both in the urban and rural, emphasize the imperatives of the same historical necessity for even more vigorous pursuit. Else, the army of the unemployed might fail to find an avocation as faster and indeed as easily as it can be available by foresting the time tested concept of khadi.

The present study aims to analyse Role of KVIC in promoting khadi and village industries over a period of ten years. The specific objectives of the study are:

— Estimate the progress in production and sales of both khadi and village industries.
— Evaluate the growth of employment and wages.
— Study the relationship between fund released by KVIC and its activities.
— Examine the share of different KVIC activities on total production.

Based on the above objectives, the following hypotheses are framed :

— The percentage share of production of khadi is less on total production of khadi and village industries.
— The growth rate of production of khadi and village industries are same.
— There is real increase of wages (at deflated value at the price level of 1988-89) in village industries and not in khadi.
— with low per capita investment K&VI activities can bring down the percentage of population below poverty line.

This study will measure the growth in production, sales, employment and wages. The tools of analysis are percentage of growth rate averages. In order to find out the real value of production, sales etc. the value is deflated using the wholesale price index. Since the study has started from 1988-89, the wholesale price index number 154.2 is taken as base year. This facilitates the researcher to find out the real value of growth. The study corner is the period of ten years from 1988-89 to 1997-98. The KVIC publishes Annual Report every year which presents all the relevant data required for this study.

Khadi and Village Industries Commission (KVIC)

After 50 years of independence and 40 years of its existence under the purview of K.V.I.C., Khadi and Village Industries are still playing a vital role in rural industrialization. 74.3 per cent of India's population inhabit in villages even today and about 6 per cent of its work force is unemployed thus under such circumstances village industries are like oasis in the desert.

Khadi and Village Industries have passed through many phases since 1923 to reach the present stage of development background.

Year	Stages of Development
1923	All India Khadi Board was set up with branches in all provinces.
1925	An Independent organization known as All India Spinners Association (AISA) was created.
1934	All India Village Industries Association (AIVIA) took shape for specific development of village industries.
1948	Akhil Bharat Sarva Sena Sangh took over the activities of both AISA and AIVIA.
1951	Khadi and Village Industries became a part of National Development Plan.
1952	All India Khadi and Village Industries became a part of National Development Plan.
1956	An act to provide for the establishment of a commission for the development of Khadi and Village industries was passed.
1957	Khadi and Village Industries Commission took over from the All India Khadi and Village Industries Board.
	Khadi and Village Industries Review Committee (1984), redefined village industries based on capital input per head of worker and location.

Classification of Industries under the seven broad categories, based on raw materials use/activities etc., are :

1. Mineral Based Industry.
2. Forest based industry.
3. Agro-based and Food Industry.
4. Polymer and chemical based industry.
5. Engineering and Non-Conventional Energy.
6. Textile industry (Excluding Khadi).
7. Service industry.

Gandhi thought of poor in villages comprising communities practicing their village arts and crafts and make village life interdependent among agriculturists and artisans. His whole plan seems to be moving round a village community with different occupation based communities depending on one another.

During the span of forty years, KVIC has endeavoured to avenues of employment for the rural artisans in their village itself from two State level khadi and village industries Boards, 242 registered institutions and 60 co-operative societies in 1957. When KVIC took over from All India Khadi and Village Industries Board, the number has reached an impressive levels of 30 State level Khadi and Village Industries Boards 4969, Registered Institutions, 30129 co-operative societies and 7.85 lakh individuals as on 31-3-1998.

The programme had taken root in 15,000 villages which has now spread to 2.50 lakh villages in 1997-98. Production which was at the level of Rs. 8.23 crores under khadi and Rs. 12.72 crores under village industries in 1956-57 has now increased to Rs. 624.10 crores under khadi and Rs. 3895.21 crores under village industries in 1997-98. The village industries under the fold of Khadi and Village Industries Commission has increased from 26 to 116 in 1997-98.

The other noteworthy feature is that the employment level increased from 15.58 lakhs in 1956-57 to 56.50 lakhs in 1997-98 of which 31 per cent were SC/ST, while women participation was about 40 per cent of the total employment.

The Board objectives that the KVIC has set before it are :

1. The social objectives of providing employment,
2. The economic objective of producing saleable articles, and,
3. The wider objective of creating self-reliance among the people and building up of a strong rural community spirit.

KVIC is changed with the planning, promotion, organization and implementation programmes for the development of khadi and other village industries in the rural areas in co-operation with other agencies engaged in rural development wherever necessary.

Production and Sales

The production of Khadi products are given in Table 21.1.

Table 21.1 reveals that production of khadi has positive growth rate, both in current and constant price level. Appreciable growth is noticed from the year 1995-96 onwards. There is negative growth rate found at constant price level, but the mean average of the same is 2.82. This low growth rate may be due to some of the following:

Table 21.1 : Production of Khadi products

(Rs. in crores)

Year	Production Rate	Growth	Production at the price level 1988-99	Growth Rate
1988-89	235.35	—	235.35	—
1989-90	257.88	9.57	240.01	2.00
1990-91	283.95	10.89	241.34	0.55
1991-92	328.62	14.93	243.86	1.04
1992-93	353.49	7.56	238.33	- 2.27
1993-94	357.28	1.07	222.33	-6.72
1994-95	389.71	9.08	218.76	-1.64
1995-96	522.23	34.00	272.24	24.49
1996-97	626.40	19.94	307.02	12.72
1997-98	624.09	0.37	292.00	- 4.90
Mean	398.10	11.89	251.12	2.81

Source : KVIC Annual Report, 1988-89 to 1997-98.

- * Immediately after independence khadi production was given much importance and there were a few village industrial activities.
- * Most of the officials, chairmen of the KVI institutions who are in charge of the KVI institutions are freedom fighters and they took much interest on production of khadi rather than VI. Further KVIC identified a few traditional village industries for their financial assistance. Khadi industry received loans at the rate of 16 per cent total production and bears no interest. Whereas village industries receives 30 per cent to 32 per cent on the basis of production value as working capital for which they interest.

It is noted from Table 21.2 that there is positive growth in the production of VI products, at current prices. The mean average of the same for ten years under study is 11.78.

However, negative growth is found for two years at constant price, but the mean average of the same is 2.70. It is concluded that real growth of village industries production for the ten years is only 2.70, whereas to khadi it is 2.81.

Table 21.2 : Production of village industries products

(Rs. in crores)

Year	Production	Growth Rate	Production at the price level of 1988-89	Growth Rate
1988-89	1443.37	—	1443.37	—
1989-90	1705.30	18.14	1587.00	10
1990-91	1994.07	16.93	1683.00	6.05
1991-92	2264.16	13.54	1680.14	-0.17
1992-93	2534.35	12.49	1701.42	1.26
1993-94	2876.58	8.34	1890.03	5.21
1994-95	3234.35	12.49	1815.57	1.43
1995-96	3504.22	8.34	1827.00	0.61
1996-97	3838.85	11.00	1907.00	4.37
1997-98	3895.21	0.13	1821.22	-4.48
Mean	2733.05	11.78	1725.6	2.70

Source : KVIC Annual Report, 1988-89 to 1997-1998.

The total production is given for both khadi and village industries. The mean average of total production at constant price level is 2.67 or 3. In the total production of both khadi and village industries, the share of khadi is nearly 13 per cent but growth rate of khadi is equal to village industries, i.e 3. The reasons for reduced share of khadi are already given. Further, in khadi production lot of working capital is locked in the form of raw materials, work-in-progress. Finished goods, conversion storage and collection cycle of khadi is longer.

In village industries, the above period is shorter and there is quick cash flow. Per capita earnings by worker in village industries will also be higher than in khadi. Hence, the share of village industries is higher in the total production of both khadi and village industries.

At present growth rate for this sector is able to provide 56.5 lakhs employment with average per capita earnings per annum of Rs. 20,000 as on 1997-98. There will be an increase of 18.8 lakhs employment for every one per cent increase in the growth rate of KVI at constant price level.

Table 21.3 : Sales of Khadi products

(Rs. in crores)

Year	Production	Growth Rate	Production at the price level of 1988-89	Growth Rate
1988-89	258.05	—	258.05	—
1989-90	291.25	13	271.04	5.03
1990-91	296.19	1.70	250.10	- 7.76
1991-92	368.96	24.57	274.00	9.52
1992-93	387.13	4.94	261.02	−4.66
1993-94	409.24	5.70	255.10	−2.44
1994-95	490.87	19.94	275.44	8.20
1995-96	567.37	15.59	296.00	7.34
1996-97	581.11	2.42	285.10	−3.76
1997-98	745.90	28.36	349.00	22.44
Mean	439.60	13.00	277.45	3.78

Source : KVIC Annual Report, 1988-89 to 1997-98.

Table 21.3 reveals that the sale of khadi is gradually increased in both the prices, but in the year 1997-98 appreciable increase of 228 crores at constant price. This may be due to the celebration of golden jubilee year of Indian independence and also allowing rebate for more than 90 days. The mean average of growth rate is 3.78.

Table 21.4 : Sales of Village Industries Products

(Rs in crores)

Year	Sales	Growth Rate	Production at the price level of 1988-89	Growth Rate
1988-89	1598.15	—	1598.15	—
1989-90	1895.48	18.60	1864.10	10.38
1990-91	2228.97	17.59	1881.26	6.65
1991-92	2526.36	13.34	1875.10	- 0.35
1992-93	2810.12	11.23	1895.00	1.06
1993-94	3232.01	15.01	2011.20	6.15
1994-95	3578.32	10.71	2009.00	0.12
1995-96	3861.75	7.92	2009.00	0.22
1996-97	4232.90	9.61	2013.12	3.06
1997-98	4319.38	2.01	2075.00	−2.66
Mean	3028.35	11.78	1914.13	2.77

Source : KVIC Annual Report, 1988-89 to 1997-98.

In the case of village industries (refer to Table 21.4) the mean growth rate is 2.77. The growth in sale of village industries is almost stable and there is no appreciable increase as in the case of khadi.

The perpendicular growth of KVI is expected one as this sector has to compete with medium and large scale and now stiff competition of this sector managed to have three per cent growth rate which is appreciable.

Production and Wage

It is needless to say that KVI activities are labour intensive. It uses simple machine and tools and employs people from rural areas who are mostly illiterate. The KVI activities are able to provide employment to the people of all ages, in case of khadi all family members including children, adults, housewives and old people contribute according to their ability. The process of pre-spinning, spinning and weaving etc., engages people of all ages. Hence Gandhiji took up this khadi activity for giving employment to the rural masses who are illiterate mostly and otherwise no work to do to earn their daily bread.

In the pre-independence period and immediately after the commencement of KVIC khadi provides more employment to the people. It was estimated that in the year 1955-56 khadi production was 76 per cent on total value of KVI production and the employment was 51.85 per cent. Further as these activities are labour intensive the share of labour on total value of khadi production is estimated from 47 to 50 per cent. The average annual per capita earning of khadi is around Rs. 13000 due to diversification of activities, and to overcome the problem of working capital in khadi sector, more village industry activities are undertaken consequently, the share of percentage of khadi and total value of production is now reduced to 13 per cent on the employment is lakhs.

Tables 21.5 and 21.6 show production of khadi and village industries on the wage paid for the same. Table 21.5 reveals that the percentage of wages on total production of khadi is around 47 per cent. It includes wages paid to spinning, pre-spinning, weaving and other processes to manufacture deflated using the wholesale index number to find out whether there is any increase in real money value. The mean average of growth rate of real wage is only 0.69 for the study period of ten years and hence it is concluded that there is no appreciable increase of wages in real money value.

In the case of village industries (refer to Table 21.6) the percentage share of labour cost on total value of village industries production is 32 per cent and the growth rate of wage at the price level of 1988-89 is 4. Hence this is real increase on the wage paid to artisan engaged in village industries activities.

Table 21.5 : Contribution of wages from Khadi Products

(Rs. in crores)

Year	Wages	% of wages on production	% Growth Rate	Wage of the the price level of 1988-89	Growth Rate
1988-89	120.28	51.11	—	120.28	—
1989-90	127.54	49.46	−3.33	119.10	−1.06
1990-91	136.74	47.82	−3.31	115.41	−3.01
1991-92	155.99	47.47	−0.73	116.10	−0.51
1992-93	168.05	47.54	0.15	113.30	−2.33
1993-94	179.32	50.19	5.28	111.58	−1.52
1994-95	190.08	48.77	−2.83	106.69	−4.38
1995-96	222.01	43.37	−11.07	119.00	11.41
1996-97	260.32	41.64	− 4.15	128.10	7.55
1997-98	270.76	43.38	4.18	126.59	−0.97
Mean	183.8	47.1	15.7	117.58	0.69

Source : KVIC Annual Report , 1988-89 to 1997-98.

Table 21.6 : Contribution of Wages from Village Industries

Year	Wages	% of wages on production	% Growth Rate	Wage of the the price level of 1988-89	Growth Rate
1988-89	426.70	29.56	—	426.70	—
1989-90	546.85	32.07	8.49	509.00	19.29
1990-91	647.31	32.46	1.22	546.33	7.33
1991-92	732.54	32.35	−0.34	543.59	−0.50
1992-93	845.58	33.51	3.58	510.13	4.88
1993-94	916.33	31.85	−4.95	510.21	4.99
1994-95	1079.29	33.37	4.77	605.84	1.28
1995-96	1135.84	32.41	−2.88	592.11	−2.27
1996-97	1271.73	32.69	0.86	623.33	5.27
1997-98	1275.58	32.75	0.18	596.40	−4.32
Mean	887.8	32.3	1.21	558.4	4

Source : KVIC Annual Report , 1988-89 to 1997-98.

The percentage share of wages on total production of khadi and village industries from 1988-89 is 3.27. It may be concluded that the average share of percentage of labour cost on total value of KVI production is around 34 per cent and the wage increase at the price level of 1988-89 for the period of ten years under study is 3.27. So, it is once again proved that Khadi activities labour intensive and it has productivity linked wage increase.

Investment, Employment, Earnings

KVI activities need less per capita investment KVIC is the major financial agent to finance the KVI activities. KVIC extends financial assistance to both KVI in the form of grant and loan. Khadi industries receive grant and loan without interest. The financial assistance consists of capital expenditure loan for acquiring of fixed assets and working capital for day to day operation in this activities. The loan issued for VI carries an annual interest of 4 per cent. In case, the above loan is not sufficient the institution can avail bank finance at higher interest rate but the difference between two interest rates will be given by KVI to the institutions under interest subsidy scheme.

The loans and grants issued to KVIC from First Plan to Eighth Plan. Its growth rate when compared to the First Plan the Second Plan is higher. Keeping view the employment potentiality, in the KVI activity, more fund was issued, during Seventh Plan. There was not any considerable increase in the allocation of fund during Eighth Plan when compared to the fund allotted during Eighth Plan. There is gradual growth of khadi production in current price and also the fund released from KVIC to khadi sector turnover of capital is found to be less than 1 in most of the years except the last two years. This is because of long duration of operating cycle of khadi sector. This is due to non-availability of stockist and executives for selling the khadi products. The marketing section is mostly reduced to rebate period of 90 days in 9 years. The khadi production also requires more time as the production process is long and further the sale of khadi is mostly on credit and it requires more collection of dues. The above reasons may be for low turnover of khadi production for the fund issued by KVIC, there is no considerable growth of khadi production. Average per capita earning per annum, under the study period is 13000, as in 1997-98 this amount is above the amount fixed by the government to define the poverty line. The government fixes the annual income, defining the poverty line is 1200 as in 1997-98. Hence it is proved that khadi industries care to elevate people above the poverty line.

In the case of village industries there is considerable fund released by KVIC and the turnover of capital is more than 4 per cent. It means that the operating cycle in most of the years is less than 90 days. It is needless to say that the sale of village industries' products is faster than khadi mostly on case basis and the conversion cycle is also less. There is considerable growth in employment during the study period. The mean average employment is 37.77 lakhs. The average of earning employment per annum is 23 per cent. It is once again proved that village industries sector not only lift people above poverty line but also provide better standard of living and handsome annual income. Both put together which generates an employment of 51.85 lakhs as in 1997-98 the average per capita earning is 20,000 the average turnover of working capital 2.6 for both KVI which is also appreciable when considering its various contributions such as low level of technology, simple machine and tools, less capital investment and competition from large scale sectors.

Another interesting point to note is that KVIC spent Rs. 1067 for creating income of 20,000. If the government and policy makers pay more attention on this sector, there will not be any problem of unemployment in rural areas and consequently, there will not be any anti-social activity.

Findings and Recommendations

With regard to progress on production and sales it is found that there is no appreciable growth perusal of production figures in current prices may reveal the growth rate. It may be clearly

Table 21.7 : Performance of KVIC in Khadi and Village Industries

S. No.	Year	K.V.I Production Values (Rs.)	Loans of KVIC (Rs.)	Turnover of capital (No.of times)	Employment (lakh in person)	Wages paid (Rs.)	Capital cost per work place (Rs.)	Annual Per capita earning (P.A) Rs. (1000)
1.	1988-89	1678.72	733.77	2.29	42.87	546.98	39.16	12,759
2.	1989-90	1963.17	826.39	2.37	46.26	674.30	42.44	14,576
3.	1990-91	2280.02	919.87	2.48	48.57	784.06	46.94	16,143
4.	1991-92	2592.79	1015.59	2.55	50.16	888.54	51.69	17,714
5.	1992-93	2876.94	1105.10	2.60	52.50	1013.63	54.80	19,307
6.	1993-94	3233.86	1171.15	2.76	52.28	1140.65	60.69	21,408
7.	1994-95	3624.06	1283.55	2.82	53.46	1269.37	67.79	23,744
8.	1995-96	4020.45	1340.28	3.00	56.72	1363.85	70.99	24,045
9.	1996-97	4516.26	1496.70	3.02	58.17	1532.55	77.64	26,346
10.	1997-98	4519.31	1522.23	2.97	56.50	1546.34	80.00	27,369
Mean		3131.65	1141.47	2.68	51.85	1076.03	—	20,3411

Source : KVIC Annual Report, 1988-89 to 1997-98.

understood that there is no appreciable growth. The reasons for the total growth rate are given in the text of the study on the whole, the real growth rate of production and sales of khadi and VI at the price level of 1988-89.

The study period of ten years is given below :

1.	Production of khadi	2.81
2.	Production of VI	2.70
3.	Production of KVI	2.67
4.	Sales of khadi	3.67
5.	Sales of VI	2.77
6.	Sales of KVI	3.00

In spite of stiff competition from handloom and large scale sector, the growth rate of employment in khadi is not negative. However, it is below 1 per cent considering the high wage component that is 47 per cent on total value of production. This sector may be given much attention to generate more employment. In the case of distribution of wages on total value of production, it is estimated that 47 per cent of total value of production of khadi go to spinners, weavers and other workers engaged in production of khadi. In the case of VI it is 32 per cent. The labour input on total value of KVI is funded at 34 per cent. So this study once again proved that KVI activities are labour intensive.

The findings on employment and wages of the study are listed below:

1.	Employment of khadi	0.55%
2.	Employment of VI	4.46%
3.	Employment of KVI	3.16%
4.	Wages from khadi	0.69
5.	Wages from VI	4.00
6.	Wages from KVI	3.27

KVIC is the major source of finance for KVI activity. The

institution may be used, retailed earnings and resources which are mostly meagre.

An average for every Rs.1067 released from KVIC, one employment in generated on the annual per capita earning is Rs. 20,000. Hence it is proved that KVI activities alone can lift the people above poverty line. It is once again proved that KVI activities do not require much capital. In the case of efficiency, of finance issued in the average turnover of capital, during the study period is 2.68. This can be increased to 4 per cent. Necessary steps are taken for marketing the village industries products.

Ministry of Rural Development and Ministry of Human Resource Development of both Central and State may have the linkage with KVIC to undertake KVI activities.

The District Rural Development Agency at the district level may be linked with Additional Director of Khadi of the district level and activities can be undertaken with the funds allotted to DRDA for undertaking various Rural Development activities.

The fund allotted under income generation may be spent for promoting village industries with the collaboration of KVIC. Linking of all the government organization under the umbrella of one organization may suddenly promote rural industries thereby more employment will be generated.

References

Fernandes, George, Minister for Defence — Khadi Institution must operate efficiency. *In Indian Express News Service,* Chennai, 7, 2000.

'Gandhiji's Constructive Programmes', *Kurukshetra,* p.12, September 95.

Krishnakumar, S., Former Union Minister "Liberalization and the Gandhi Test", *The Hindu,* August, 15th, 2000.

KVIC Annual Report, 1988-89 to 1997- 98.

Neelamegham, R., "KVIC as a Poverty Alleviator", Khadi Gramodyog, *Journal of Rural Economy.*

N.N., Chabra, Rural Industries, March, *Kurukshetra,* Vol. XIVI, No. 5, February, 1998.

Shrivastava, S.K., A Study on Rural SC/ST Entrepreneurs, *Kurukshetra,* May, 2000.

INDEX